Sauna Constructi

Liability Disclaimer

The publisher and/ or author take no responsibility for the consequences of applying the information found in this volume. Before building your sauna, make sure your materials, sauna layout & design, and equipment will be installed in accordance with local laws, zoning rules, requirements, and sound construction techniques. If in doubt, consult a local licensed architect and/or civil engineer. Make sure the build stays within the terms of your insurance (if applicable). For the electrical system, please hire a professional and licensed electrician. Faults in electrical systems can cause serious health damage or even death.

Legal Notice

Please note that information contained within this document is for educational and entertainment purposes only. All effort has been executed to present accurate, up to date and reliable, complete information. No warranties of any kind are declared or implied. Readers acknowledge that the author is not engaging in the rendering of legal, financial, medical or professional advice. The content within this book has been derived from various sources, please consult a licensed professional before attempting any techniques outlined within this book.

For more information, email: contact@homemadesauna.com

First Edition
Kraków 2024

ISBN-13: 1978-83-972969-0-9

If you have questions or need help,
please get in touch.
Thanks, Wojciech Kumik

https://homemadesauna.com/

CONTENTS

INTRODUCTION

Construction may be tricky without the right guidance. Good planning, preparation, tools, knowledge and materials are key to success. Lacking any of these can lead to delays, quality issues, and other problems.

This guide will teach you the basics of the construction of a small sauna. It will not cover every aspect involved. There are many things to consider. These include soil types, wood types, heater types, and manufacturers. Also, there are local laws, regulations, construction techniques, standards, and climate zones. A sauna built in Florida will probably differ from the one built in Canada, where temperatures drop as low as 0°F (-20°C) frequently. Everyone also has their individual needs in terms of functionality. Some will be fine with a small 4' x 6' (1.2 m x 2 m) sauna. Others will want a large, three bench level sauna. It may have a vestibule, an internal shower, a changing room, and an office. We attempt to offer general guidance here, but ultimately it's up to the builder to plan the construction and research local materials and suppliers.

This guide is aimed at an average person who is not a carpenter and who only has basic experience with construction (or no experience at all). For this reason, some of the details shown here might not be of the highest level. My goal will be to teach you how to go from zero to a sauna, even if you've never built anything like that in your life. We will skip the fancy dovetail and half-lap joints. If you are an experienced carpenter, feel free to improve the design described here.

The sauna that we'll build will be based on my own design. A 2-bench level sauna with a hot room dimensions of 6.5' by 6.5' (2 x 2 m) and around 7.5' high (230cm). The sauna will have a small 3' (90 cm) changing room/vestibule. This is a tried-and-true design that is popular and works well. It is a good compromise between a bare-bones sauna and a big sauna with additional spaces and features.

How Do I Use This Book?

This book is divided into five chapters. The first chapter, 'Sauna design principles' deals with the key things that are needed to build your sauna. Use it as a reference during your build to get specific knowledge on individual areas of construction. It's also useful if you want to do a design that is different from the one explained in this book. The second chapter: 'Preparation for construction' is about getting started with your build. It covers the things you should know before construction starts. The third chapter, 'Sauna Building' is designed to guide you through the construction of the shell of the building by explaining each step in detail. The fourth chapter is 'Sauna interior'. It will help you navigate the process of building the interior. At the end of every subchapter, there will be an ACTION - a detailed instruction that you can follow to help you build your sauna.

If you just want to start building, you can start at chapter three, but if you lack the experience, I'd recommend reading all chapters.

Why Build Your Own Sauna?

By building your own sauna, you can save a large amount of money on labor costs. You can also customize it to your liking, choose the materials you want, and the heater that matches your needs. It is also a great adventure! You will learn the basics of construction, and you can tell your friends about it! Warning: Your friends might ask you to build a sauna for them. If you succeed in building your own sauna, you will get a deep sense of satisfaction every time you use it. If you build it right, it will last for years and might even outlive you. Your kids will thank you for it!

Because you bought this book, it means you probably know to stay away from barrel saunas. Rightfully so. Most barrel saunas are poor quality. Over time, the timber dries out, and the gaps between tongue and groove boards start leaking air. Countless stories and cries for help are online. They come from sauna owners whose barrel saunas don't get hot after a few years of use. Another reason is that the shape of the barrel sauna doesn't allow for two bench levels. This is a big red card. Even when there are no leaks, this layout will cause you to experience sub 150°F (65°C) at the most, at the bench level.

The Origin Of Sauna

While Sauna is a name that comes from Finland, similar 'hot rooms' have been built by different cultures over thousands of years. They take different forms and names. Slavic cultures have banyas. The Turkish gave us Hammam. The Nordic countries have Saunas. The Native Americans had 'sweat lodges,' and the Celtic tribes had beehive-shaped sweat houses, 'Teach Allais' in Irish. Then, there are mixtures of these. They were created when two cultures collided. This resulted in countless subtypes and interpretations. They have different room layouts, heat, humidity levels, and traditions surrounding them.

This book is concerned with the construction of a modern interpretation of a sauna. If we were to be strict with what the Finnish standard calls for, we would have to make the sauna about 8' (2,5 m) high internally, and it would feature a wood-burning stove. This setup is not always optimal, as we will discuss in later chapters.

A traditional smoke sauna viewed from the exterior.
Source: https://www.duminuke.lt/en/smoke-sauna/

The sauna capital of the world, without a doubt, is Finland. In fact, in 2020, Finnish sauna culture was included in the World's intangible cultural heritage list by UNESCO. There are approximately three million saunas in Finland, a country of five-and-a-half million people. Sauna culture there is long, and it's a big part of Finnish culture. The original saunas built in Finland, well before the invention of electric heaters and continuous fired heaters, were so called 'Smoke Saunas'. They were heated by a single fired heater. A heater with large amount of stones was fired up and brought up to a temperature. After it was sufficiently hot, the smoke from the building was released and the sauna could be used. The walls had a permanent black appearance from the smoke. I can only imagine the beautiful aroma of Nordic spruce of pine in there!

The sauna build that we'll follow over the course of this book is a modern interpretation of a sauna - a design that is fit for modern times and preferences. I will use an electric heater, but a modern wood fired heater can also be used.

Sauna Construction & Use Safety

Before you begin locating, building, and using your sauna, it's important to talk about safety.

A sauna is built to promote wellness, and it should not be the cause of harm, whether during construction or use.

Construction is many times more dangerous than a typical desk job. You will encounter dangerous tools, heavy materials, and risky heights. If you lack the experience, you might not even know the danger is there until it's too late. Don't rush things, and use the Personal Protective Equipment that's fit for the job you are doing.

Fire risk

There are tens, if not hundreds, of sauna fires all over the world every year. Take every precaution you can to limit the risk of fire. Locate your outdoor sauna away from any existing or planned building and away from any combustible materials. Do the research and check your local building code for fire safety distances.

The sauna heater manufacturers always provide safety distances from the side, front, and back of the heater. In most heaters, there is a minimum distance of 3.5' (110 cm) from the top of the heater to the ceiling. Take particular care with wood stoves and the chimney. It's best to use a special sauna chimney system supplied by the heater manufacturers. Make sure the chimney goes through a wall while respecting minimum distances to combustible materials. It's a good practice to use non-combustible materials all around the heater. Fiber cement board, bricks, tiles, and natural stone are all decent materials that provide fire safety when mounted in proximity to the heater. Fires are classified by the type of material that's burning. In the context of a sauna, we will need a fire extinguisher that covers ordinary materials like wood and electrical equipment. Ideal for this is a dry powder fire extinguisher, as it covers both cases: an electrical fire and a wood fire.

Sauna use safety

The sauna room door should always open outwards. The door should have a simple spring roller or a magnetic locking mechanism. Never install a lock that can prevent someone from leaving the sauna. Always hydrate before the sauna and leave if you feel unwell. Don't pressure anyone to stay any longer than he/she wants to. Before using a sauna, it's good to consult a doctor, as using a sauna can have adverse effects on you if you have blood pressure, skin, or heart issues.

CHAPTER 1
SAUNA DESIGN PRINCIPLES

This chapter is designed to give you general knowledge of sauna design, with the most often asked aspects described in detail.

Sauna refers to a standalone sauna building, a sauna *room* (inside a building), and a verb. In this book, we will mostly use the first two options.

What Should Be Inside a Sauna Building?

A hot room is a fundamental component of an outdoor sauna. However, there are other functions that go well with a sauna, and they could be included.

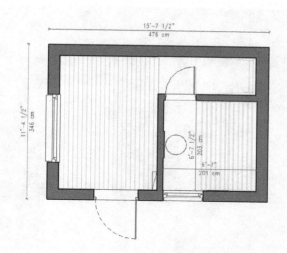

Example of a sauna layout that has a generous changing room, a shower and a hot room measuring around 6.5' x 6.5'

Changing room /vestibule

This add-on is the most common one. Even a small changing room allows you to leave your coats or towels out of the rain. A changing room also acts as an airlock - it prevents the heat from escaping when you enter a sauna. If you are considering anything more than the basic hot room sauna, then pick this add-on.

Shower

If you have a space and budget for it, consider installing an internal shower inside. It is an excellent addition because after each sauna session, you need to cool down, and the best way to do it is with cold water. External showers are also an option, but not everyone likes to shower out in the open because of privacy issues or bad weather.

A shower right next to a sauna is a great addition and a touch of luxury. Source: Author's own photo.

Lounge

Lounge space is a great addition if you have the space for it. It is essentially a larger vestibule. Actually, the only thing I regret about my first sauna build is that I didn't make the lounge space bigger. This space can be used for sauna parties, reading books, meditation, and even for emergency sleeping when you have guests over. Falling asleep with the smell of timber is an experience on its own. The Lounge can also act as a changing room. If you install a foldable desk, it can be a perfect place for remote working.

Toilet

A toilet is an obvious possible addition, but it is not common. It is easy to understand why. People usually build their outdoor saunas fairly close to their homes. The added complexity of dealing with sewage pipes is not enough to justify building a toilet in their saunas. If you are planning a commercial sauna build, then this is a must - have. You can integrate it into the sauna building or build a standalone facility nearby.

Cold plunge

This can be either outside on a patio next to the building or inside. Some people repurpose chest freezers so that they can cold plunge even in summer. There have been many options that popped up recently, with countless companies offering plastic or metal cold plunges. I prefer to go the traditional way. You can buy an old barrel or a metal stock tank and fill it up with water. Replace the water when necessary. One issue is with water freezing over, but there are solutions to that. You can either keep the water above freezing temperature with an external heater or add salt to it. Keep in mind that the cost of salt might be higher than the cost of water replacement. It is also not environmentally friendly to dump salty water into the environment. It has to be disposed into the sewage system

Hot bath

A Jacuzzi-style large bath, usually round. Although not strictly necessary, it adds to the overall 'spa' experience'. Some People prefer an outdoor hot bath over a sauna, and by having one you are catering for those people. This can be placed inside or outside. If placed outside, it can act as a cold dip in the winter. A hot bath is a good addition, but it is not entirely necessary if your main focus is just a sauna. If your hot bath has any kind of water filters/water pumps, make sure to drain them before winter to prevent ice from damaging them.

External space next to a sauna can play a big part in creating an inviting and relaxing environment.

Space requirements

Optimize the sauna interior based on the number of users that will use the sauna. On average, a person takes 2 feet (60cm) of bench space. By measuring the total length of usable sauna space, we can get a rough number of possible users. Below are a few examples.

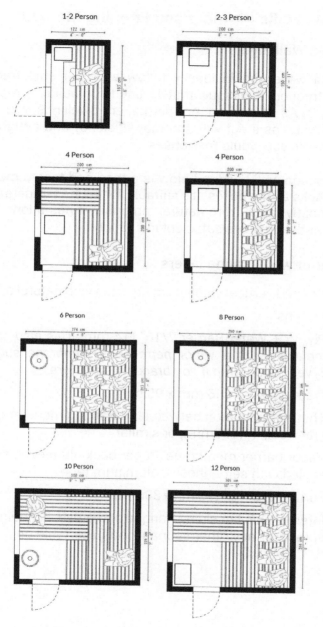

Plan view of different sauna sizes. Dimensional requirements for different capacities.

Sauna Walls - Timber and Framing Method

Sauna Wall layers

Sauna walls should ideally follow a proper stick-framing construction technique that is used for building modern houses. As saunas are not permanent dwellings, you don't need to be as strict with thermal efficiency and airtight envelope as you would for houses.

The sauna wall buildup below is a tried and tested method that ticks all the boxes. It's suitable for sauna temperatures, it's mostly made from natural materials, it has a long lifespan, and it provides sufficient insulation.

Exterior wall - sauna layers

1. Charred vertical shiplap siding, oiled with natural oil 3/4"
2. Battens
3. Ply Air + Water Barrier 7/16" (14 mm) *This also can be replaced with a vapor permeable membrane such as Tyvek house wrap if you brace the structure.*
4. Framing, 2"x4" (45 mm x 95 mm)
5. Thermal insulation between the framing members, Mineral wool, 4" (100mm), or similar
6. Vapor barrier membrane, Paper back aluminum, seams sealed with self-adhesive aluminum tape
7. Furring 1/2" - 1" (15 mm- 30mm)
8. Internal ship lap siding: tangue and grove, Scandinavian spruce, or any other sauna wood (see table on p.91)or 5/8" (14mm)

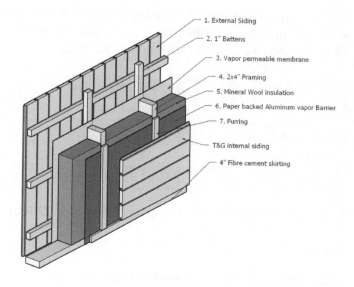

1. External Siding
2. 1" Battens
3. Vapor permeable membrane
4. 2x4" Framing
5. Mineral Wool insulation
6. Paper backed Aluminum vapor Barrier
7. Furring
T&G internal siding
4" Fibre cement skirting

Axonometric diagram showing different wall layers in an outdoor sauna

Timber sizes

Timber sizes have been standardized to simplify designing and building. You can either get a rough-sawn timber - timber that has been cut, or you can get planed (dressed) timber, and this is what I recommend. It is slightly more expensive, but it's usually already dry, straight, and without splinters. It will make construction work easier. We will distinguish between two measurement systems: imperial and metric.

Imperial

Why we distinguish between nominal and actual? The commonly used 2×4 lumber actually measures 1½ x 3½ inches, a result of historical compromises in forestry and construction. As demand for lumber grew, especially post-Industrial Revolution, the need for standardization emerged, leading to the current naming convention. The lumber industry prioritized efficiency and uniformity, which ultimately reduced the actual size of the 2×4. Understanding this discrepancy is important, as it highlights the economic compromises that shaped modern construction practices.

Nominal	Actual
2" x 4"	1 ½" x 3 ½"
2" x 6"	1 ½" x 5 ½"
2" x 8"	1 ½" x 7 1/4"
2" x 10"	1 ½" x 9 ½"

Timber usually comes in Lengths of 8, 10, or 12 feet.

Metric

In Europe, C24 timber is used. C24 means that the timber is classified as suitable for construction: it has a low moisture content, dimensional stability, and a certain strength rating. It comes in standard profile dimensions. Different lengths are available, so check your local lumberyard.

Metric (mm)	Imperial
45 x 70	2" x 3" equivalent
45 x 95	2" x 4" equivalent
45 x 120	
45 x 145	2" x 6" equivalent
45 x 170	
45 x 195	2" x 8" equivalent
45 x 220	
45 x 245	2" x 10" equivalent

What timber size to pick?

If you are building a small sauna that is below 6' x 6' (182cm x 182cm) or if you have limited space, you can consider going with 2x3" timber (45mm x 75mm). Anything equal to or larger than 8 x 8' - you should be using 2" x 4" (45mm x 95mm). If you live in a freezing climate or your sauna is larger, then you should probably go with 2x6 timber (45 x 145 mm).

Wall framing

Wall framing refers to a technique of creating walls with timber studs. A stud is a single vertical timber structural member. The spacing of the studs is usually every 16" (40cm). This is dictated by the width of sheathing panels, which come in 4 feet by 8 feet (in Europe and Australia 125cm x 250cm). Each wall is made from the bottom plate, studs, and top plate. The studs and other framing members can be attached together by a framing nailer (expensive and fast). You can also use a cordless drill and screws (slower and cheaper). The third option is traditional nails (slowest, cheapest, and needs more skill). In most cases, the cordless drill and Torx wood framing screws offer a good balance of speed, affordability, and ease of use.

Wall opening framing

To install a door or window, you will need to make a wall opening. The framing around the opening should allow the loads from the roof to be transferred through the wall. If you skip this part, you are risking the window cracking, not being able to open the door or window, or a structural failure. You will need a structural beam called a 'header' that will transfer the vertical loads. The framing around the window will transfer the loads down to the subfloor and the foundation. There are a few intimidating names in framing: King, Jack, and Cripple. These are the names of individual framing members that are used when framing a window. The main thing is that the header takes any weight from the top plate and transfers it down through the jack studs and down to the bottom plate. Below is an example of window framing, shown in an elevation.

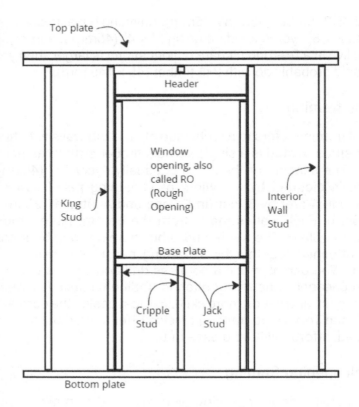

Top plate

Header

Window opening, also called RO (Rough Opening)

King Stud

Interior Wall Stud

Base Plate

Cripple Stud

Jack Stud

Bottom plate

Elevation view of window framing

Common window header sizes:

Window size	Header
3 feet or less	Double 2x4
4 feet 6 inches to 3 feet	Double 2x6
5 feet 9 inches	Double 2x8

Corner Framing

When two external walls meet in a 90-degree corner, the studs have to be positioned in a certain way. This layout leaves space for insulation and minimizes cold bridges in corners. In the example below, wall A Extends to the corner, and there is an additional stud rotated 90 degrees that is nailed beside the last stud. That rotated stud acts as an additional surface for nailing the last stud of Wall B. It also provides a nice backing for our internal paneling.

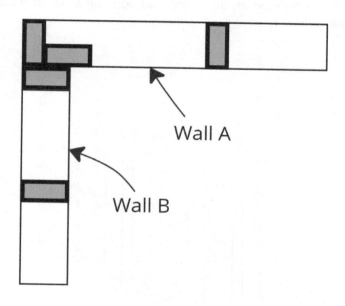

Detail plan view of 2 walls joining at a 90-degree angle

Lateral stability of a timber wall

Walls that just use nails or screws are quite weak when it comes to lateral strength. Lateral strength is the 'side to side' movement of a structure. In timber framing, every connection is considered a pivot. If you don't use something to overcome that, your building will have limited lateral strength, which can cause it to sway with the wind.

There are 2 main ways of achieving lateral strength.

A traditional way is through the use of bracing. Bracing means that angled timber is introduced to the structure. The timber used can be 1" x 6" (30mm x 150mm), and it works best if it's cut into the frame tightly. Usually, it is at an angle of 45 degrees. It is a good and inexpensive method of strengthening, but it requires some skill and time. It also does not provide an air barrier, so you will have to do that separately.

Axonometric view of a wall with cross bracing

Another way is through the use of structural sheathing. The structural sheathing is when you use a sheet material that is nailed on the inside or the outside of the structure. Sheathing material usually comes in 4' x 8' in North America and 125 cm by 250 cm in Europe and Australia. Historically, the most often used material was OSB (Oriented Strand Board). It has one drawback - It is not permeable. This means it does not let moisture move towards the outside easily. It is crucial for the wall to be able to 'breathe.' Moisture builds up in the walls and can cause rot and timber swelling.

Today, there are better material options. In North America, Zip system sheathing is often used. In Europe, Siniat produces a product called Defentex. Both options provide Continuous Air and water barriers as well as structural rigidity (lateral strength). Keep in mind that these materials can be quite heavy (Defentex is 15 kg/ sq m) and expensive.

Sauna Ventilation

Sauna ventilation is one of the key ingredients to an excellent sauna experience. If you experience a sauna without any ventilation, as is often the case, you will feel a big difference compared to a ventilated one. We often exit the sauna because of stale air, not because of the heat. It is not only a matter of fresh air. Ventilation is also needed to properly mix the air in a sauna. Hot air rises to the top; cold air falls to the bottom in a sauna. The temperature difference can be as high as 100°F (40°C), and this can be definitely felt by sauna users. A good ventilation system can help to decrease this difference by mixing the air.

What is Löyly?

The best sauna air is a mixture of fresh hot air and some water vapor, known as "Löyly". It is measured on a relative scale, from zero % to 100%. It is measured relative to the air temperature, because the greater the temperature, the more vapor can be 'stored' in the air. In other words, it is a measure of the actual amount of water vapor in the air compared to the total amount of water vapor that can exist in the air at the current temperature. In a Finnish sauna, the relative humidity ranges from five to fifty percent. The humidity is raised by pouring water on the heater's rocks. For a small sauna (8-10m³) one to two cups of water is enough

Sauna ventilation has two main forms. They are mechanical and natural (gravity-based). In a mechanical ventilation system, the fresh air enters the sauna, mixes with hot air, and then is extracted by an electric mechanical fan. Some fan manufacturers have special fans designed to be used in saunas. In natural (gravity) ventilation, laws of physics are used to exchange the air. The choice of which system to use should be carefully determined based on the heater type (wood or electric) and sauna location (internal or external).

For the amount of fresh air that's needed, I'd recommend looking at the ventilation requirements standards in your country.

Every sauna user should have a fresh air supply of at least 20m³ per hour. The 20m³ value comes from comes from the polish building code. The finnish building code calls for air to be echanged 3 to 6 times per hour which will give a similar values. If you are scratching your head right now, you are not alone. The complex calculations can be usually substituted by a rule of thumb if you are building a private sauna: 100mm air vents and a mechanical fan with speed control set to lowest setting. If you throw a sauna party with lot's of people, just turn up the speed.

Mechanical Ventilation

- Used with Electrical heaters.
- Used with wood heaters that are fed from outside the sauna room.
- INTAKE: located centrally above the heater, about 2' up from the top of the heater.
- EXHAUST: Mechanical fan located on a wall furthest from the heater, about 1' (30 cm) from the ground.

- DRYING: This is an extra exhaust with a valve that allows it to be closed. It is opened when the sauna does not provide natural ventilation.

The VTT Technical Research Center of Finland conducted a series of experiments on a small 2 m x 2 m x 2 m sauna to test different intake and exhaust placements for optimal heat distribution. The most optimal configuration was for the fresh air to be brought in by a vent placed about 2' (50 cm) above the top of the heater. The exhaust should be below the level of the foot bench. For this configuration to work, you should equip the exhaust with a mechanical fan, preferably with variable speed control.

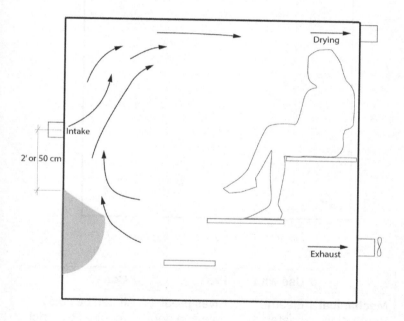

Mechanical ventilation diagram

Natural (gravity) Ventilation

- Used with wood heaters that are fed from the sauna room.

- It can be used with electric heaters, but you will get more temperature layering.
- Use this method if you want just a functioning sauna and don't want to overthink it.
- INTAKE: Either through gaps in the floor board (this is often used in Finland) or by an air channel under the heater.
- EXHAUST: Air duct located on a wall furthest from the heater, about 8" (20 cm) from the ceiling.

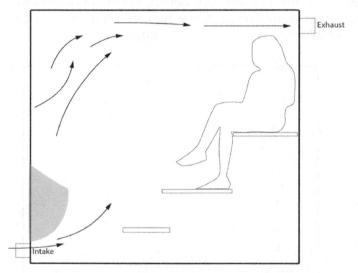

Natural (gravity) Ventilation diagram

	Use with	Pro's	Cons
Mechanical Ventilation	Electric heater	Gives predict-able and good ventilation,	It can be noisy, requires electrici-ty, and costs more to install

Natural Ventilation	Wood heaters, electric,	No electricity is required, and it is simple to install	Prone to changes in atmospheric pressure, leads to greater heat layering

Ventilation in homes with a mechanical, heat-recovering ventilation system

This book is concerned with outdoor saunas, but mentioning the ventilation in indoor modern saunas is worthwhile. In Europe, the energy efficiency regulations require the new homes to be fitted with Heat - recovering mechanical systems. Spaces that people use should have either a fresh air supply or an exhaust. The air is carried through pipes, usually hidden in ceilings and walls. The fresh air comes in from outside, goes through a heat exchanger that preheats the air from outside, and is transported where it's needed. The exhaust ducts take the air from the bathrooms and kitchen and go through the heat exchanger before being exhausted from the building. The whole system requires an airtight building. Indoor saunas are usually located in bathrooms, which have exhaust ducts. The fresh air comes in under the bathroom door and then is extracted by the exhaust duct in the ceiling. The sauna should take fresh air from the bathroom, and the exhaust should also be in the bathroom. This is because for ventilation to work properly, you must ensure the mechanical exhaust fan creates no negative pressure. It's also not a good idea to exhaust air straight into the house's ventilation system, designed for lower temperatures and humidity levels.

Heat Source

There are many different types of sauna heaters and too many to list all types, subtypes, and brands. The heaters can be divided by the energy source. The most common energy sources for sauna heaters are electricity and wood. There are also gas-powered heaters, but they are more suitable for large saunas because of the initial cost. In this book, we will focus on electric and wood heaters. Several subtypes of heaters developed over the years, each with its own characteristics.

Electric heaters:

- Standard heater
- Mesh heater
- Pillar heaters
- Heat storing heaters

Wood-burning heaters:

- Basic heaters
- Mesh heaters
- Single-fired wood heater

Electric Heaters

The electric heater consists of resistance heating elements. A large current passes through the heating elements, and they have an electric resistance; as an effect, they heat up. Think of it like the heating elements in your electric oven. Electric sauna heaters are becoming more popular. They are clean and convenient and allow you to use the sauna without the firewood preparation. They are an obvious choice in urban areas. This is because some countries and states impose strict rules on particle emissions and solid fuel energy production. Electric heaters are always paired with a controller - internal or external. It works like a thermostat - you set a desired temperature, and the heater is turned on and off to maintain this temperature. A temperature sensor is necessary for this to work properly. Heater manufacturers always specify the recommended location of the sensor- it is usually close to the ceiling. An external controller is a good thing - it saves the electronic hardware from the high temperatures of the sauna environment. The external controllers can be Wi-Fi enabled. They allow you to turn on and off your heater from anywhere. For this to work, you will need a Wi-Fi connection - either by a signal from your house or a Wi-Fi repeater.

Electric heaters come in single-phase or three-phase configurations. The single phase is your regular wall outlet electricity, and the three-phase is the type of connection for more power-hungry devices. It requires a thicker cable with 5 wires inside, one for each of the three phases, a neutral, and a ground wire. I strongly recommend getting a three-phase heater. It allows you to install a much higher power heater.

Sizing an electric heater for your sauna

A general rule for sauna heater size is a 1-meter cube of internal volume (1m x 1m x 1m), which should be paired with 1kW of power. For any uninsulated surface like glass window or door, you should add another 1kW per 1m2.

Example:

A sauna room 2m wide, by 2m long, by 2.2m high = 2*2*2.2 = 8.8m³

We have to add a glass door: 0.6m x 1.8m = 1.08m

8.8+1.08=9.88

The heater power should be around 10kW.

If you want faster heat times, you can get a slightly bigger heater, e.g., 11kW. If you have windows in your sauna, they, of course, contribute to a greater heat loss, but with modern double or triple-argon-filled glazing, the heat loss is reduced significantly.

Can I install a smaller heater, say 4.5kW if my optimal size is eg. 9kW?

If your optimal heater size is e.g. 9kW, but you can only accommodate say 4.5kW, then I would add a bit of extra insulation. The heater may struggle to maintain the temperature during the sauna session, and may be constantly turned on. As a result, this can cause premature heating element failure.

The sauna described in this guide will have 8m³ of volume, one standard sauna glass door, and a large, 2m x 2m window. If we follow the above calculations, we will get a 13kW requirement, but from experience, I know that 9kW would be sufficient and 11kW would be optimal.

An Estonian manufacturer's HUUM model DROP electric sauna heater. Source: huum.com

Harvia's electric sauna heater - model cylindro. The heater is quite tall, but the wooden floor has been raised, leaving a penetration for the heater. Source: https://www.harvia.com/en/sauna-references/

Wood Fired Sauna Heater

The most basic type of sauna heater is a standard wood-fired heater. It stands on the floor, has a medium capacity of rocks, and sometimes has a glass window in the firebox door. The heater works pretty much like a fireplace, but its shape, size, and the place for rocks make it especially suited for saunas. There are also mesh wood heaters. This type of heater has mesh walls and exposes a lot of the rock volume. It can hold significantly more rocks than normal heaters, so the heat-up times are slower, but there is more heat energy stored in it.

	Electric	Wood-burning
Pros	Simplicity Energy efficiency Effortless Fewer emissions	Off-grid ready Helps with ventilation Renewable energy source High power
Cons	Requires adequate electricity connection Heating elements are sometimes prone to wear out.	Emissions Laborious Heat adjustment is less precise

Pros and cons of different types of heaters

We will use a 9kW electric heater and a natural (gravity) cross-ventilation solution for our build. It is the simplest and most accessible solution. The heater will be hung on the wall, so it will take up little space. Many manufacturers have heaters of this type, so I will let you pick which one to get. I suggest choosing a heater with good local support for any future issues.

Harvia's wooden heater. The toned matte charcoal finish and large tempered glass on the fire chamber door suits modern aesthetics. Source: https://www.harvia.com/en/sauna-references/

CHAPTER 2
PREPARATION FOR CONSTRUCTION

> *"You can use an eraser on the drafting table or a sledgehammer on the construction site."*
> *— Frank Lloyd Wright*

Sauna Budget

Prices of materials differ by location and by market fluctuations. Also, when writing this book (2024), construction material prices are rising due to demand, inflation, and supply chain issues. For this reason, it is impossible to accurately predict the price of sauna construction. The best and most accurate way is to calculate the cost based on raw materials quantities and local labor costs. Make sure you add 10% of any material as wastage and off-cuts.

It can help to create an Excel spreadsheet listing the material name, quantity, the quantity increased by 10%, material cost, and total cost. You can also add things like a hyperlink to the online shop, a tick mark (acquired yes/no), and a comments section. Generally, try to keep this simple.

If you are building the sauna yourself, skip the labor cost, but remember you will have to spend your own time building the sauna. I assume you are ok with that since you bought this book.

Factor in things like paying a qualified electrician to wire up the connection. Remember about the cost of clearing the land and any earthworks. Hiring a digger is a great time and back saver. If you want a quick way of judging the construction price, research the national average home construction cost. The figure might be a bit off, but it will give you a ball-park figure. At the time of writing this, the price per square foot in the USA is around 250 USD. From my experience, the material cost is from 100 to 200 USD, depending on the materials you choose.

Locating Your Sauna on Your Land (or Water)

If you own the land, you will build on it, and you are probably the expert in this matter. But if you are building for a client or have the freedom of choosing a place to build, here are a few things to look out for.

A few questions that you might consider when choosing the location:

- **Do you have any good views?**

   Orient your sauna to take advantage of it and add a big window. Consider privacy also

- **What access is available?**

   Will future users be able to access the sauna easily? What if someone with limited mobility will want to access the sauna?

- **Soil type**

   Is the soil load-bearing? What is the soil composition? Will you need perimeter drainage?

Land boundary

Check local regulations to see how close you can get to the fence. Are there any natural lakes or nature reserves with setbacks?

The slope of the ground

Does your foundation need to factor in the slope? Where will the entrance be? Will you need steps? How many steps? Will you need the railing to be code-compliant?

Is there Wi-Fi signal available?

If you plan to control your sauna heater remotely, you will need an internet connection.

Can you run an electrical cable to this location?

Check the distance to your electrical box and speak to a local electrician.

Will you need planning permission?

Speak to your local authorities and ask if you will need planning permission. This is usually determined by the square footage of your sauna and the zoning laws. Most US states are either under 200 or 120 sq ft.

Distance from your home/cabin

Are there any fire regulations that might restrict you from building the sauna?

Are there any zoning rules that make it impossible to build?

Is the building site accessible by truck? (for bringing tools and materials)? Is it within a crane's reach?

Is there a crane rental that is in your location?

The more you research, the smoother the build will go. Try to answer as many questions as you can.

Tools Required

Saunas are usually made with timber, and this is what we will focus on. For timber, the tools you will need are:

- Cordless drill
- Circular 6.5" saw
- Staple gun
- Hammer
- Measuring tape
- Spirit level
- Woodworking bar clamps
- Spade
- Shovel
- Screwdriver set
- Spanner set
- Metal shears
- Carpenter's pencil

A 'nice to have' tools:

- Framing nailer
- Finishing nailer
- Concrete mixer
- Laser level
- Track saw
- 'Sawzall' / reciprocating saw

How to Read Architectural Plans?

Plans that are part of this book are simplified versions of full architectural plans. The plans contain all the information that's necessary to successfully build. The main drawing is the plan view. It is a top-down view that shows the building as if it was sliced with a knife horizontally. It contains information like wall framing dimensions, internal layout, and section lines. Sometimes, different symbols reference other views. Other views supplement the design. They include external and internal elevations, foundation, ceiling, roofing plans, and electrical and plumbing plans. They also include detailed section drawings and any other drawings with unique design information. Every project is different, so the list of drawings can also vary.

Architectural drawings can be rendered at various scales, depending on the information presented and the overall size of the structure. A scale of 1:50 indicates that one unit on the drawing represents 50 units in real life. In Imperial measurements, scales are often described using actual units, such as ½"=1'.

For sauna construction, scales like ½"=1'-0" or 1:50 are commonly employed due to the typically compact nature of saunas, which usually occupy less than 200 sq ft (18m²). These scales provide an appropriate level of detail for such small structures.

A title block, typically located at the bottom or right side of the drawing, contains essential information about the document. This includes the drawing name, number, scale, project name, and revision number. Additionally, you may find special notes providing general guidance on interpreting the drawings. It's crucial to thoroughly review all this information.

Dimensions on architectural plans are generally shown to the faces of framing members, facilitating the wall framing process. Not every wall stud requires dimensioning; only key elements such as "T" wall junctions or the start and end of a wall need to be specified.

Always pay close attention to textual information on plans. Some details are more effectively communicated through text, so notes are often incorporated directly on the drawings, above the title block, or within the plan itself. These notes can provide critical insights and instructions that may not be immediately apparent from the visual elements alone.

Safety

Construction can be quite dangerous, especially if you have never done it before. Protect your body with all possible means because it's the only one you have. Be extra careful with power tools. Use PPE (personal protective equipment). Look at all the warning signs when using any chemicals and follow the safety protocols. It is only your responsibility to make sure you do yourself no harm.

CHAPTER 3
SAUNA BUILDING

> *"Construction is the art of making a meaningful whole out of many parts. Buildings are witnesses to the human ability to construct concrete things."*
> — Peter Zumthor

Site Preparation

Mark out a rectangle roughly 1' (30cm) larger than your sauna will be. Check the diagonals (measurement between opposite corners) and make sure they are exactly equal. This way, you know the rectangle has right angles.

Remove the topsoil with a shovel to a depth of around 4 to 6 inches (ca. 15 cm). If you have access to a digger, then take advantage of it. Level the site if possible. Remove any existing plants or roots that may be in the ground.

Services

Electricity

Dig a 2' (600 mm) to 3' (900 mm) deep trench to run your electric cable, depending on your local regulations. The electricity will be needed for light and heat (if you end up going with an electric heater) and possibly the exhaust fan. If your sauna will be right next to your house, digging might not be necessary. Just secure an electric cable inside a protective sleeve to your building's external facade. Be extra careful not to damage the cable.

Water

If you plan to build a shower inside your sauna, dig a separate trench for the water pipe. The depth should be larger than the frost depth for your location. This depth generally increases the further north you are. In the US, it ranges from 0" to 100" (mm). It's a good idea to keep some distance between the electric trench and the water trench so that if something breaks, you can easily dig up the right one without breaking the other. PVC pipes are the most common because of their durability and cost-effectiveness.

Place your cable/pipe at the bottom of the trench and cover it with about 1' (25 mm) of sand. Place a plastic colorful tape and fill it up with dirt. The plastic tape will help to prevent accidental damage if somebody digs in the same place in the future.

Run the services to the exact spot where they will be needed inside the sauna. Take photographs where the cables are run for future reference.

Gray water

If you choose to build a shower in your sauna, you must dispose of the used water. Connecting to an existing septic tank/sewage system is the best way. If this is not possible, you could use a dry well, also called French drain. It is a hole in the ground that transfers water into the ground. It's best done by digging a hole about 4' (120cm), placing a round perforated pipe, 16" diameter (40cm), and throwing clean gravel around it. The pipe and the gravel will help to slowly release the water into the ground.

Warning: Make sure your local authorities allow the use of dry wells and that they are compliant with environmental laws in your country. Never use dry wells to dispose of toilet water. I would not recommend using soap in the shower if you have the dry well, only rinsing. A dry well is ok to use to dispose of relatively clean water. It is not a sewage system and, if used inappropriately, can contaminate the ground. In some countries, it is illegal, so check your local building code.

Run a PVC water pipe from the location of your drains into the dry well. Make sure the pipes are sloping down to the well.

This is a photograph of the construction of the sauna Tuula. On the bottom left, we can see the drainage pipe from the hot room, and on the right, from the shower. In our design, there is no shower, so you can skip that.

Sauna Foundation

There are many ways to do a foundation for an outdoor sauna. The correct one should be selected based on the soil load-bearing properties, materials available, complexity, frost depth in your area, and the building weight.

The foundation should always sit on undisturbed soil. This is because soil settles over time, and freshly dug-up soil is not able to support the same weight as settled soil. Usually, a period of 5 years is needed for the soil to settle. If you have a slope, excavating the soil and filling it in after the foundation has been built is better. Frost depth is the depth at which the ground can potentially freeze. This depth is different in every location. Check the IBC (International Building Code) in the US or a building code in your country.

The IBC has an exception to the frost protection rule. "A free-standing building with an area of 600 sq ft (56 m2) or less for light-frame construction, with an Eave height of 10 feet (3048 mm) or less and assigned to Risk Category I (temporary buildings or those with few occupants)". Long story short, most saunas fall under this definition, so don't stress the frost depth too much.

Pier Foundation

A pier is a vertical column made from concrete. This is done by digging a round hole and placing a cardboard tube that will be later filled with concrete. It is probably the most common type of foundation for small structures. It is relatively easy to build but requires high accuracy. I usually specify this type of foundation in sauna projects.

Pier and Pad Foundation

This is just like the Pier foundation, but there is an additional concrete pad underneath each pier. The pad is usually three times wider than the thickness of the pier. This type of foundation is good for heavier structures.

Pad foundation

A basic, easy to build type of foundation. It consists of a flat piece of compacted ground, and concrete is usually poured to make a stable base. Reinforcing the concrete with steel is a good idea, as it will give it extra strength.

Ground screw foundation

A less common type of foundation that uses round steel tubes screwed into the ground. It is one of the fastest ways to do foundations, but it requires a special driver with proper torque to drive the ground screw into the ground. Good for sloped ground.

Concrete block foundation

One of the most basic types of foundation. This foundation is constructed by placing concrete blocks on a bed of compacted gravel, ensuring they are perfectly leveled. The timber floor joists rest on the concrete blocks. Timber and concrete needs to be separated by a waterproofing layer, because concrete will soak up water from damp soil and over time it will cause the timber to rot. You can use an EPDM or Asphalt based membrane.

ACTION

Tools:

- Spirit level
- Marking out a rope
- Spade
- Mechanical ground compactor (optional)
- Digger (optional)

Materials:

- Crushed gravel, enough to fill 8 holes 18" deep (45 cm)
- 8 concrete blocks
- Adjustable post base (optional)

Mark out the exact location of your sauna with a thin rope. Pick one of the foundation types that is the most suitable to your own situation. If in doubt, speak to a local builder.

We will use a concrete block on a crushed gravel foundation for this guide. It is suitable for most ground conditions. It will result in the sauna's first floor being elevated from the ground by about 18" (45cm), so make sure you are ok with it. If you have a sloping ground, the floor might be even higher, and you might need to build a few stairs.

Dig 8 holes, about 18" deep (45cm), in the marked-out locations. Fill the holes with crushed gravel and compact it. You can use a motorized petrol or electric compactor or a manual compactor. Place large concrete blocks in the 8 locations. The bigger, the better, but make sure you can move them - concrete is heavy. Make sure the top of the blocks are perfectly level with each other.

If you have a sloping site, then you can get an even level by adding more concrete blocks.

Fine adjustments can be made by adding or subtracting crushed gravel or using an adjustable post base with a "U" type of attachment.

After the services and the foundation are done, cover the ground with 2" (5 cm) of sand to level the ground. Next, lay down a geotextile membrane (fabric sheet used in construction and civil engineering to improve soil stability and drainage) that will stop any plants from growing. You can use steel pegs to secure the membrane. Cover the membrane with another 2" (5 cm) of clean gravel. It will hold the membrane down securely and give you a nice-looking surface under your sauna.

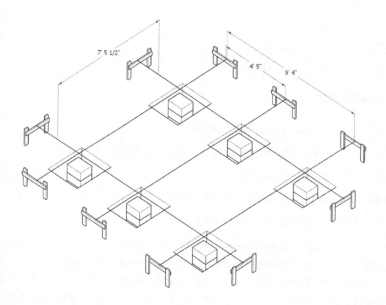

Axonometric view of concrete block foundation & marking strings set up

Sauna Subfloor

The sauna subfloor provides a stable surface to raise your sauna on. It is essentially a timber floor, which is insulated and has penetrations for any services needed. The subfloor in our design is done on-site, which means each timber floor joist is assembled individually in its final location.

ACTION

Tools:

1. Timber saw
2. Measuring tool

3. Pencil
4. Battery drill.
5. Screws
6. Stapler
7. Sheet metal scissors
8. Clamps 12" (30cm)

Materials:

1. 2x5" (45x145 mm) timber
2. Metal mesh for animal control, 5x5mm, stainless steel
3. Rock wool insulation
4. Vapor permeable membrane.
5. OSB boards, ⅝" or 18mm

Create a perimeter frame out of 2x6" (45x145 mm). Make sure the frame is perfectly level. Check if the angles are square by measuring the distance of the opposing corners. They should be exactly the same. Inside this frame, distribute the floor joists at 16" in the center (40 cm), which means that from the center of one joist to another, it should be exactly 16" (40cm). It's important because the OSB we will use later comes in standard sizes, and we want the edges of the OSB to land on a joist. Put blocking between the floor joists. Blocking is short pieces of timber that go perpendicularly to the main floor joist. They help to stiffen up the floor and prevent the joists from twisting.

The bottom of the floor should be secured against animals with stainless steel mesh. You can also use plywood, but it's a more expensive option.

The metal mesh, should be made from stainless steel and the mesh should be approx. ¼" x ¼" (5mm x 5mm). Cut sections of the metal mesh, the length should correspond to the space between two longer floor joists. The wight should be larger by 2" (50 mm) on each side. Bend the two 2" tabs upwards. They will be used to secure the mesh to the floor joists with a stapler.

With the mesh in place, the Vapor permeable membrane should be installed. Use long sections and start at the edge of the floor. Use a stapler to attach it to floor joists.

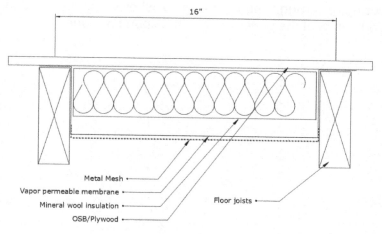

Section view through the floor build up, without the finished floor materials.

Next, cut the mineral wool insulation to size - the width should be slightly larger than the space between the floor joists. If you use a rigid mineral wool, it will hold it's shape and because it's slightly larger than necessary, the friction will hold it in place. Its good idea to position it up from the mesh, so that the rodents have a harder time getting to it.

Next, line the space between the joists with a vapor-permeable membrane. You can use a continuous piece that goes up and over the joists. Make sure to tape the membrane seams with a special tape for this purpose. Place the 4" (100mm) Rock wool insulation between the floor joists, making sure you cover every bit of space. Don't forget about plumbing penetration and electrical cable.

Chapter 3 | Sauna Building

Place the OSB on top of the floor structure, and secure it with screws every 8" or 20cm. If you use nails, the floor might end up squeaky. Don't forget about plumbing penetration. The plumbing should be finished with a Gully. A gully is a device similar to a P trap. It creates a water seal and prevents foul smells from coming up through the pipe. The electric cable should also come up through the OSB. Both should come up through the OSB exactly where they are needed. You can seal the penetration with expanding foam.

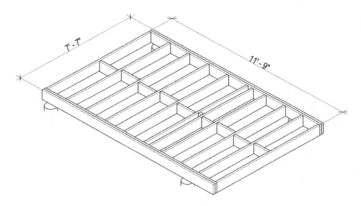

Axonometric view of the floor frame built on top of the foundation.

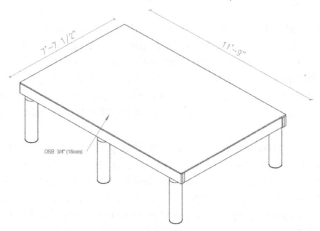

Axonometric view of the OSB subfloor

Detail of the prefabricated foundation with adjustable beam base and the floor joist. The Timber has not been attached yet with screws.

Framing

Now that we have a stable platform to work on, you can take the next step. Framing is by far the most enjoyable step in sauna construction. You go from a simple deck to something that resembles a building in a matter of a day or two. The finished result of this step will be a frame of the building. A 'bare bones' skeleton that will support all the other bits and pieces that make a sauna. The important thing here is to watch out for dimensions and accuracy. The principles are easy, but some things can make this part difficult. Timber that is not perfectly straight, small mistakes that pile up, non-co planar studs: these mistakes will make building the sauna more difficult down the road. We will start with walls.

Walls are usually built flat and then raised into a vertical position. This way is much easier and allows for greater accuracy than if we were to frame the walls vertically. If you are not fully confident with this part, get help from an experienced carpenter.

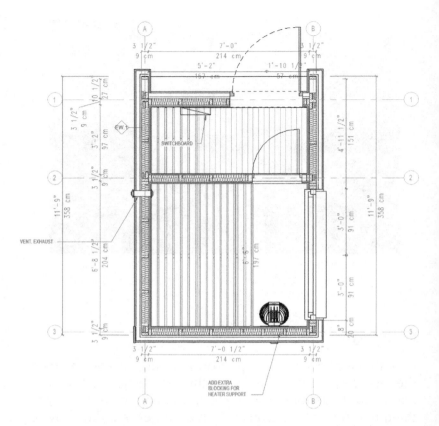

The sauna we are building is based on the HMS Eevi model.
A link to PDF download can be obtained at the end of this Ebook

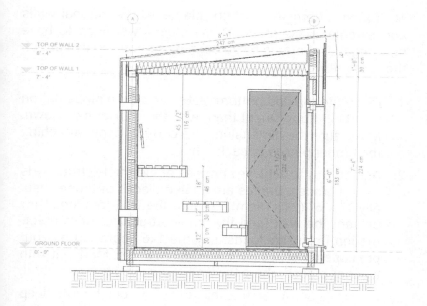

*The section drawing. This layout features 2 full benches and a 12"
(30cm step). You can also skip the step and make the sauna height
smaller.*

ACTION

Tools:

- Battery drill
- Measuring Tape
- Spirit level
- Torx Screws

Materials:

- 2x4" (45mmx95mm) studs

Start by looking through your plans (if you have them) and
analyzing them. Every wall will have a bottom and a top plate.
There will be wall studs between them, usually spaced every

16" (40cm). Remember about places where internal walls and external walls meet. These places will need to have blocking that's rotated by 90 degrees so that you can attach the external walls to it.

1. Place the top and bottom plate and all the studs flat on your OSB floor. Orient them with the shorter side down. Make sure the dimensions are correct. Begin attaching the timber pieces to each other.

2. A good way to achieve stiffness of the whole structure is to add braces. Braces are angled pieces of timber, usually 1" x 6" (2,5x15cm), cut into the wall framing. They prevent the wall (and the whole structure) from deformation from side loads. Lay the 1x6 board flat on your pre-assembled wall at a 45-degree angle. Mark out with a pencil places where the wall studs need to be notched.

3. Cut 1" (2,5cm) (or the thickness of your board) deep groves using a circular saw inside the pencil line. Cut additional groves between the two lines. Watch out for any screws!

4. Using a chisel, remove the timber between the two external cut lines. Ensure the board fits tight and is flush with the wall's surface. This task takes some skill and patience, but you will get a hang of it quickly. The tighter the board fits, the better the stiffness of the wall will be.

5. Secure the board with one or two screws at every board-stud overlap.

6. Raise the finished wall into position and secure it with a temporary brace. Use screws to attach the wall and the floor together. The screws should be long enough to go through the bottom plate, the OSB, and into the rim joists.

Axonometric view of first wall raised into position

A temporary brace can be used for the first wall.

1. Continue the process by building, raising, and securing all the external and internal walls together.

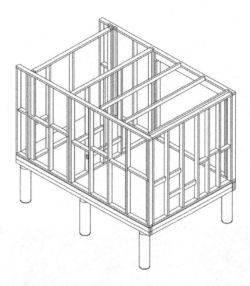

2. Place another top plate on top of the walls so that the end overlaps an adjoining wall. The top plate will help to stabilize the whole structure.

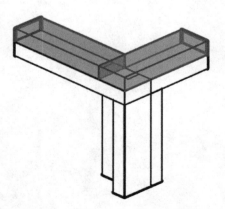

The two highlighted top plates overlap the 'bottom' top plates at corner connections.

3. For the windows, you will need to create a rough opening (R.O.) to suit the window size you want. Make sure to use a proper framing technique using king studs, cripples, sill, and trimmers. Use a proper header to transfer any loads from the roof.

4. Sauna benches need to be supported by additional blocking. It is necessary to take the weight of the bench and the people sitting on it. Add a vertical 2x4"(4.5cm x 9.5cm) blocking between two wall studs at a height where your wall hanging benches will be. In our design - 24" (60 cm) and 42" (106 cm) on both side walls of the sauna. Make sure you mount the supports where the bench frame will be, so measure down from those dimensions. Measure the height from your finished floor level, not from the subfloor. If your floor is not yet finished, then just add the thickness of the flooring material you will use. Double-check the height because it can't be changed easily later. In our case, the finished floor will be about 1.5" (4 cm). If you want, you can also wait until the rough-in stage for the installation of bench blocking.

5. Create a short 1' (30 cm) wall on one side of the sauna. The wall should be above the window (check the sectional drawing on the previous pages). This wall will create a pitch to our roof. Since we have a double wall plate in place, we can't really nail these studs from the bottom. Use 90-degree metal connectors instead. Space the studs evenly, every 16" (40 cm) on the top of the wall, where the big window is.

6. Place another 2"x4" 'top plate' to finish off the little wall. Ideally, you should add a cross brace to stabilize the structure. Cut the ends of a couple of 2x4 studs at a 45-degree angle and fit them between a top plate and a few 'little' studs. Attach them with screws. Now, the framing is almost complete. The last thing to do is add the roof structure.

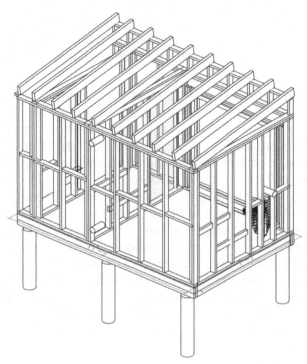

Axonometric view of first wall raised into position

Home Made Sauna's model Tuula being built.

Sauna Roof

The roof structure should be designed with a couple of factors in mind. Things like location, possible snow load, and span of the roof will determine the waterproofing materials and the structural layout of the roof.

As a rule of thumb, use 2x6" (95x145 mm) spaced every 16" (40 cm) on center. If your location gets extreme snowfall or if you are planning a green roof, then go with 2x8" (45x195 mm) rafters. These thicknesses are a rough guideline for a moderate snow load of 50 PSF and small spans of around 8-10 feet (2-2.5 m). The table below shows different maximum rafter spans depending on spacing, wood type, and nominal size.

Nominal Size	Spaced (o.c.)	Species/Grade			
		S. Pine	Doug. Fir	Hem-fir	S.P.F.
		#2 grade	#2 grade	#2 grade	#2 grade
2" x 4"	12	9-0	10-0	9-8	9-10
	16	7-9	8-7	8-5	8-6
	24	6-4	7-0	6-10	6-11
2" x 6"	12	13-6	14-7	14-2	14-4
	16	11-8	12-7	12-3	12-5
	24	9-6	10-4	10-0	10-2
2" x 8"	12	17-1	18-5	17-11	18-2
	16	14-9	16-0	15-6	15-9
	24	12-1	13-0	12-8	12-10
2" x 10"	12	20-3	22-6	21-11	22-3
	16	17-6	19-6	18-11	19-3
	24	14-4	15-11	15-6	15-8

source:https://www.mycarpentry.com/rafter-span-tables.html

The roof usually has a sheathing layer, similar to the wall sheathing. A standard thickness here is 5/8" or 18 mm. The most important layer is the waterproofing. There are different options, but my favorite is a double continuous Asphalt roofing membrane applied with a torch. The roof is often sheathed with OSB or a structural but breathable material (see the next subchapter).

The roof can be waterproofed in many ways. The table below shows the advantages and disadvantages of a few more common materials. In our build, we will pick

EPDM roofing membrane is a good way to go, although it is slightly more expensive. Otherwise, I would use a continuous asphalt roofing membrane or a standing seam metal roof.

ACTION:

Tools:

1. Battery drill
2. Measuring Tape
3. Spirit level
4. Torx Screws

Materials:

1. 2x6" (45x145mm) studs
2. OSB ⅝" (18 mm)
3. Drip edge
4. Gutters
5. Standing seam metal roofing
6. Underlayment - Ice & Water Shield or asphalt bitumen roll
7. Asphalt roll nails or bitumen adhesive

The roof framing for our build should be made from timber beams: 2x6" (95x145mm) or 2x8" (95x195mm). The 2x8" should be used in locations with substantial winter snow load.

The roof rafters should be spaced every 16" (40 cm). They will be angled, so they should be notched at a correct angle in places where they meet horizontal top plates. Use Hurricane ties to secure the rafters to the top plate. Hurricane ties are an easy and good method of adding extra structural strength to your sauna's roof. Another way is to use long rafter screws, screwed in through the top plate, upwards into the rafters. Use a 5/8" (or 18 mm) OSB sheet to make a continuous sheathing on your roof. The edges should always support the OSB sheets. The sheets should have an expansion joint of about ⅛" (5 mm), so make sure you leave this gap where two sheets meet.

Use ice & water shield underlayment or a bitumen asphalt roll to waterproof the roof. Research these materials and use the correct installation methods. As a final layer, Install standing seam metal roofing. Get pieces of roofing cut to the needed length by the manufacturer or the seller. Start with one side and continue to the end of the roof.

Vapor Permeable Membrane

The next step is to seal the structure from the outside. Why? Because you don't want a change in weather to soak your timber structure. This step can be done in about two hours with 2 people and a ladder.

An air barrier is needed to prevent wind from blowing into your insulation. The barrier needs to be breathable. Imagine the difference between wearing all polyester clothes on a hot day and breathable cotton or linen clothes. The cotton stops most of the air but allows the vapor from your skin to evaporate. Houses and saunas are similar. The walls need to breathe. Since the 1980s, people have been using house wrap or roofing membranes to achieve this. It is a relatively inexpensive and easy to apply product. One thing is that it can rip easily, so get a heavy duty reinforced product. All the joins must be sealed with special tape to provide a continuous membrane. The membrane can be attached with a staple gun to the framing temporarily, and when it's all in place, you can use 1"x0.5" (2,5x1,27cm) battens screwed in vertically to the framing to secure it further. Start from the bottom of the structure so that the top parts overlap the bottom. A self-adhesive tape appropriate for the membrane should seal the membrane joints. When you reach the windows, apply the membrane - you will cut openings later. The membrane should tightly envelop the whole building, including the roof and the joins between the wall and roof.

To cut window and door openings, use a box cutter/utility knife and cut Horizontally on top and bottom of the opening angle from the corners of your openings.

Use peel & stick flashing tape such as FlexWrap from Tyvek (or similar) to flash the window and door openings. You need to make sure the water does not get in.

When installing the vapor-permeable membrane, always start from the bottom. The overlap will cause any water to be directed outwards.

Ventilated Facade and Roofing

When our sauna is wrapped in a roofing membrane, it's initially secured only by staples, which can easily come loose with even minor weather changes. To ensure a more robust attachment to the building, we'll install vertical shims, approximately 1"x1" (2,5x2,5cm), at every stud location. These shims will not only hold the membrane tightly in place but also provide a solid foundation for the facade installation.

Before proceeding with the vertical shims, however, we need to consider a potential issue: the ventilated facade could inadvertently create a cozy habitat for rodents, which is certainly undesirable. To prevent this, we'll install a 90-degree, 2"x2" (5x5cm) stainless steel mesh profile at the wall's base. Using a stapler, temporarily attach the mesh at the level where the bottom of your siding will be. The vertical shims will then be installed over this, securing the mesh firmly in place.

This approach ensures both the stability of the roofing membrane and protection against unwanted critters, setting the stage for a successful facade installation.

Metal mesh on the bottom of the ventilated facade should be installed before the vertical shims

Installation of wood shims on the roof that hold the roofing membrane down. This ladder is probably a safety violation - do not follow it!

Now, we could install the external siding if we wanted a horizontal board orientation. Personally, I prefer vertical orientation. To achieve that, we will need another shim layer, this time horizontal, spaced every 16" or 40 cm. The shims will allow the timber siding to 'breathe' at the backside. Any moisture will evaporate through the gap created by the two shims.

The roofing can be done similarly. In our sauna, we put well charred and oiled spruce boards as an experiment. The boards we installed were pretty wide - around 8" (20 cm), so eventually they bowed. This created an uneven surface and gaps between the boards. For this reason, we eventually replaced it with standing seam metal roofing. It has a lifespan of around 50 years. Metal roofing is sold by suppliers that will get you everything you need, including flashing, screws and the roofing itself. Every system is slightly different, so ask your supplier on the best way to install the roofing,

The external facade boards are being installed.

Chapter 3 | Sauna Building

ACTION

Tools:

- Mitre Saw
- Battery drill

Materials:

- 1"x1" (3x3 cm) laths, around 430 feet (130 m)

1. Cut 4" (10cm) strips of stainless steel wire mesh. The length should be sufficient to go around the outside wall. Bend the mesh in half at a 90-degree angle. Attach the wire mesh with a staple gun to the bottom of the wall where the siding will be.

2. Cut 1"x1" (2,5x2,5 cm) shims to size from the level of the wire mesh to the top of your wall. Attach them vertically with screws and cordless drill. They should be in every stud location. Go around the whole sauna.

3. The 1"x1" (2,5x2,5 cm) should be attached horizontally, starting from the bottom all the way to the top of the wall, in 16" (40cm) increments.

Charred and oiled facade boards have a great looking natural look.

How to prolong the life of wood?

Wood is a natural material, and most wood species are not resistant to rot and fungus. The main problem is with wood exposed to moisture - rain and snow.

You can treat timber in many ways to prolong its life. The internal siding in a sauna room can be treated with natural preservatives like paraffin oil, but this is unnecessary if the users meet proper hygiene standards.

On the other hand, the preservation of timber facades should be carefully considered. One way is with the architecture it-self - by the use of overhangs. Overhangs are part of the roof that 'stick out' from the building and keeps the rain away from the wall. Two feet (60cm) overhang will help massively.

There are also chemical and physical ways to preserve wood. The table below shows just a few of the ways that can be used. Do your research to see which method suits your wood of choice. Some methods can be mixed together. Others can be applied only to specific timber types.

	Advantages	Disadvantages
Pressure impregnation	Durable	Can contain harmful chemicals
Charring of the surface	Natural, no chemicals involved	Cost
Plant-based oil	Cheap, natural	Needs to be reapplied
Pigmented lacquer	Cheap	Needs to be reapplied
Thermal modification	Durable	High cost

Shou Sugi Ban (or Yakisugi) is a Japanese wood preservation method worth mentioning. It translates to "burned cedar." It is an old, tried and tested technique that creates a burned texture on the surface. Furthermore, it is a natural way of conservation and, if done correctly, can be very durable. The treated wood is resistant to Fungi, rot, insects, and UV light to some degree. It has been successfully used on different wood species: Spruce, Larch, Cedar, Pine, and Accoya.

Cedar and Larch are recommended for use outdoors because of their durability. When you apply the Shou Sugi Ban technique, they will be even more durable. To increase the charred board's longevity, putting a coat of Natural oil, such as Linseed oil, after installation is a good idea. This should be repeated every 10 to 15 years, and more often on the sides exposed to the sun. Manufacturers of Yakisugi boards also advise varnishing the wood to further protect the wood from rain and UV rays. This will save you on maintenance resources.

How do you get a gray-looking timber?

If you prefer a natural 'old' gray-looking timber, there are several ways to achieve it.

One way is simply to expose the wooden boards to UV rays. This method does not give consistent results, and the side not exposed to the sun will remain unchanged. You are also risking mold and rot.

This method can be used on Thermally modified timber such as Thermo Pine, but the results will also be inconsistent. On the other hand, the building will have its own character that's influenced by the environment it sits in.

Another way to get a gray appearance is by using Iron Sulfate staining. Some wood species that contain tannin, a chemical compound naturally occurring in plants, will turn gray when exposed to sulfur oxide. This reaction takes some time, but it's independent of UV rays, so you can achieve a uniform color. Wood can even be sealed with a clear varnish - the chemical reaction will still happen. Some wood species that this method can be applied to are larch, cedar, oak, walnut, mahogany, and cherry. Pre-staining woods that are low in tannin with a solution of tannic acid will produce results similar to woods that are naturally high in tannin.

CHAPTER 4
SAUNA INTERIOR

> *"The bitterness of poor quality remains long after the sweetness of low price is forgotten."*
> — Benjamin Franklin

Now that the exterior shell is almost finished, you can step back and look at all the progress you have done. You have an almost complete building. All that's needed to fully enclose it are doors and windows. When you enclose it, you can take your time doing the interior, as the work is not dependent on the weather. This is an important milestone that you should be proud of achieving.

Sauna Doors and Windows

Sauna doors are generally narrower than standard doors. This limits the amount of heat escaping when the door is used. Ordering a prefabricated door is the easiest and most cost-effective way to get your door. There are many sauna door suppliers of sauna doors in most Western countries. They come complete with a Glass or wooden door, door frame, and hardware. Always measure the RO (Rough opening) for the door when ordering the door. The RO should be about ¼" to ½" (8 to 15 mm) wider and taller than the door. The gap allows you to install the door. Wooden or plastic wedges are useful for temporarily securing the door frame.

Attach the wood frame with screws; usually, they come with the door. If you place small shims in the gap between the food frame and the wall framing, your door frame will rest on them, held by the screws. Use expansion tape to fill the gap between the opening and the door frame and make it airtight with Aluminum foil self-adhesive tape applied inside the sauna where the door frame meets the wall. Use the same material as your internal paneling to trim around the door.

Standard US sauna door dimensions:

Door Size	R.O.
24" x 80" (Standard)	25" x 81"
28" x 80"	30" x 82"
30" x 80"	32" x 82"
32" x 80"	34" x 82"
34" x 80"	36" x 82"
36" x 80" (ADA handicapped)	38 ½" x 82"

Standard Metric sauna door dimensions:

Door Size	R.O.
69 x 189 cm (Standard)	71 x 192 cm
69 x 199 cm	71 x 202 cm

The doors can be bought from one of the sauna-specialized shops. They usually come in three designs: Full glass, wooden with a small window, and a full solid door. By buying the complete sauna door, you can save a good bit of time. The external door could also be bought, but I see the value of making a custom one here. You can make the external siding and the door material match exactly. The effect can be well worth it. A uniform material between the door and the siding makes the exterior look consistent and almost seamless.

The inside of the door can be made from Plywood, and on the outside, you can use Tongue and groove siding to get a clean look. I recommend buying the door hardware (hinges, door latch, and a handle from a sauna equipment supplier.

ACTION:

Tools:

- Timber wedges
- cordless impact drill

Materials:

- Prefabricated door
- expansion tape

1. Pre-assemble the door frame if it comes in pieces.
2. Position it in place in the Rough Opening.
3. Use timber wedges to fill the gaps. The vertical parts of the door frame should be perfectly plumb.
4. Use Torx screws to secure the door frame to the rough opening studs.
5. Fill the gaps between the opening and the door frame with expansion tape. The tape will help to keep the heat inside the hot room.
6. Seal the gaps with self-adhesive Aluminum tape.
7. Trim around the opening on the inside and the outside. Use ½" (1,27 cm) thick timber paneling with the tongue and groove cut off.

Installing Windows in Your Sauna

Professional Installation vs. DIY

When it comes to installing sauna windows, getting some help is a smart move. Many window suppliers offer installation services, which can save you a lot of hassle, especially with larger, heavier windows. If you decide to go the DIY route, be prepared for a bit of a workout – those big windows can be quite a challenge to handle on your own.

Window Specifications

Frame Material

For sauna windows, wooden frames are the way to go. Other materials just don't cut it:

- PVC: Deforms at around 176 °F (80 °C)
- Aluminum: Expensive and a great heat conductor, which isn't ideal for a sauna

Glass Type

Tempered glass is a must. It can handle the high temperatures and sudden changes in heat that are common in saunas. Regular glass is likely to crack, which is the last thing you want.

Glazing Options

- Double or Triple-Glazing: These options help with heat retention and prevent moisture condensation inside the sauna.
- Tempered Layers: While only the innermost layer needs to be tempered, it's wise to temper all layers to avoid any mix-ups during installation.

DIY Installation Methods

If you're up for installing the windows yourself, you have two main options:

Custom-Made Windows: Order windows that meet all the necessary specifications.

DIY Construction: Design and build the window yourself. It's doable, but be ready to add an extra week or two to your project timeline.

The installation process for windows is similar to that for doors, so if you've handled a door, you should be able to manage a window.

Electrical Stuff

Saunas are centuries-old traditions that were invented way before electricity. But nowadays, a sauna without electricity may be too unrefined for most people. Even if your sauna is off-grid, you can install a photovoltaic-powered system with a battery and light the sauna this way. If you install a wood-fired heater, connecting large power is unnecessary. You only need the electricity to run LED lights and maybe speakers. The power demands are much greater since we are building a sauna with an Electric heater.

Single-phase heaters and three-phase heaters are available. Without getting too technical about electricity, we need to know that single-phase heaters generally have lower maximum power and three-phase heaters can have larger power. In fact, single-phase heaters go up to 3.6 kW only (Harvia make 4.5kw for some locations).

To determine the heater power needed to reach the sauna temperatures, you have to calculate the volume of your sauna room.

Assume 1 kW of heater power for every cubic meter (or 35 cubic feet (1 m³)) of the sauna.

This handy formula tells us that if our hot room is 282 cubic feet (ca. 8 m³), we will need a heater with about 8kW of power. In addition, for every uninsulated surface, you have to 1kW per meter squared (or 10 square feet (0.93 square meters)).

The window and the glass door will amount to around 3.5 meters squared (or 37 sq ft).

That means our ideal heater should have around 11kW.

It is not a strict rule. If it's cost-prohibitive, you can also go with 9kW, but 11kW will get you the best results. Our sauna is well insulated, and the window glass is double-glazed, so the heat loss will be small. Depending on your heater, the controller can be internal or external. The external controllers are usually installed near the entrance to the hot room. They tend to last longer because they are not exposed to heat and humidity.

Light in your sauna

The electricity will also be used to light the interior. The hot room will be lit with a waterproof LED strip mounted behind the backrest. This location is ideal, and I have tested it in my own sauna. The backrest provides a good mounting place for the LED strip. It hides the strip, meaning no glare, and if the LED strip is aimed at the back wall, the light will bounce nicely off the wall and into the room, giving a nice, soft light. In my experience, this lighting is entirely sufficient. A dimmable switch should be connected to the LED. It will allow you to adjust the light based on the mood you want to go for. Make sure your sauna LED is waterproof - ie. it has rating of IP65 or better.

The changing room only requires a single, ceiling-mounted LED point light. The porch / external light is optional. If you decide to install it, it will be another small LED light with a waterproof enclosure.

Electrical Plan

The electricity enters your sauna from the ground, penetrates the floor in the changing room, and goes directly into an electrical breaker box. This breaker box will be in a central location and will distribute electricity to the other components. The power comes straight into GFCI, then out from the GFCI goes to circuit breakers linked with light, heater, sockets, etc.

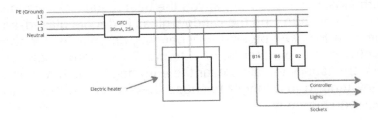

Rough electrical plan outline. A more detailed version should be developed based on the heater manufacturer's guidelines.

ACTION:

The description and steps below are only for general guidance. Please hire a professional electrician. You can cut costs by doing some work for him, like installing the electrical boxes, but a professional should do the wiring and safety checks.

Tools:

- Electrical pliers
- Electrical screwdriver

■ Insulation stripper

Materials:

■ Electrical switchboard

■ GFCI (Ground Fault Circuit Interrupter),

■ 3-phase circuit breaker for the heater (Use the one with proper current capacity. For example, 16A for 9kW heater)

■ 1 phase circuit breaker for lighting (6A)

■ 1 phase circuit breaker for socket (10 A)

■ electrical boxes for light switches,

■ aluminum waterproof linear LED enclosure,

■ 40' (12 m) silicone cables 1,5 mm2 for lights (3 wire),

■ 19' (6 m) silicone cables 2,5 mm2 for the 9-kW heater (5 wire)

1. Install the electrical boxes in place. The light switch should be at a comfortable height of around 4.5 feet (135 cm) above the ground level. The boxes should extend beyond the stud to accommodate the thickness of the tongue and groove paneling.

2. Drill the holes for the wires. Use a ¾" (1.9 cm) spade bit and locate the holes in the center of the 3 ½" (8.9 cm) stud. I like to drill the holes at a height of around 1' (30 cm)

3. Do the Electrical switchboard wiring following the electrical drawing. (If you are not familiar with electrical jobs, get an electrician to do it for you)

4. Check wiring insulation with an insulation resistance meter. (At this stage, your switchboard is not energized yet)

5. Check GFCI operation with the dedicated meter. This step is critical, so don't skip it. You need a special meter that electricians have. I would highly recommend

getting a certified electrician for this job. If the GFCI doesn't work properly, you are risking your life. This is critical to your safety in the sauna.

Note: Leave some extra bit of wire at the heater connection to make it possible to move the heater aside and replace heating elements if they burn. I keep some extra heating elements as a spare.

A tidy electrical system is a safe electrical system.

Sauna Ceiling

The ceiling in a sauna ideally should be flat. Its purpose is to limit the height of the hot room, so the heat stays where it can be usable. Use 2x4s to create a ceiling structure, one rafter at either end of the ceiling and two or three in between. The best way to attach the beams is with beam hangers - a special metal hanger designed for this purpose. In the pictures below, you can see that we installed the ceiling after the wall paneling, but it would also have been good before.

ACTION:

Tools:

- Cordless impact driver

Materials:

- Beam hangers
- 5 pieces of 2" x 4" (45 x 95mm) beams. Length should span the ceiling.
- Torx screws
- Paper backed aluminum foil
- Internal paneling
- ½" -1" (15-30mm) Shims

1. Measure the distance between two opposite walls, where the ceiling will be. Take measurements in 3-4 locations. Hopefully all dimensions are the same. Subtract ⅛" (3mm) from that dimension. This will be the length of your ceiling beams.

2. Cut the beams to size

3. Attach beam hangers on both walls. The height is pretty important, since this will determine your finished ceiling height. Refer to the section drawing for the height.

4. Install the beams in beam hangers, securing them with torx screws.

5. Optional: You can use Nylon string woven around and between rafters to support mineral wool. Nylon is safe to use in sauna temperatures.

6. Use staple gun to secure the Alu-papaer vapor membrane. Make sure to tape any seams.

7. Attach wooden shims to the ceiling beams

8. Use a staple gun to secure internal ceiling paneling.

Installation of the ceiling rafters

Finished ceiling ready for paneling

Insulation

When all the services are installed, you can get started with insulation. It is essential to retain heat and improve the energy efficiency of your sauna. With the rising energy prices, it is a no-brainer for me. The initial cost of insulation is small when compared to the overall cost of the building. Some people have successfully made decent saunas without any insulation, but these saunas are either made of solid wood or used as tent construction. Solid wood construction requires much more timber and provides worse insulation than mineral wool. The sauna tent is a temporary structure, and we are building something that will last for years.

The best insulation for an outdoor sauna is, without a doubt, mineral wool. It is superior in price and performance to other insulating materials. The insulation thickness is chosen based on the thickness of the wall studs. Generally, a 4" or 100mm thick insulation is adequate for most locations. If you live in a cold climate, consider 6" (150 mm) studs and insulation. Do not use Expanded Polystyrene Foam (Styrofoam) under any circumstances. It is not made to withstand the high temperatures of a sauna and can cause off-gassing of harmful chemicals. One exception to this would be the sauna floor. The floor sees much lower temperatures than walls or ceiling. The risk of off-gassing is much smaller because of this.

Insulation is measured with R-values in North America and U-values in the Metric system.

In residential construction, the insulation thickness is determined by the climate zone where the building is constructed. Mineral wool has an R-value of about 4 per inch, so 3 ½" (9 cm) mineral wool will have an R-value of about 14. Is this sufficient? In my opinion, it is if you are a casual sauna user and use it only a couple of times a week. For the ceiling, I would like to install a 3 ½" or 4" (10 cm) inch mineral wool insulation between the ceiling joists and then another layer that goes perpendicular to the first layer. This gives us a total of R32.

What about climate zones? If you live in climate zone 7 or plan to use your sauna commercially, I will consider bumping up the R-value to about 22. A 2x6 wall with mineral wool in the studs will satisfy this.

Don't overthink the insulation. We are not building an energy efficient home that will need a Passive House Certificate, so we do not have to stress about it too much. Sure, your sauna will not be super-insulated, and you will spend a couple of dollars more in energy costs. At the same time, we should keep in mind the point of diminishing returns - after a certain point, the investment made will not yield big enough returns to justify it. I believe a standard 2x4 with 16" (40 cm) on center studs and 4" (10 cm) of mineral wool insulation is exactly that - entirely sufficient.

ACTION:

Tools:

- Long knife for cutting mineral wool
- Staple gun

Materials:

- 4" thick mineral wool. Width should be slightly bigger than space between wall studs

1. Place the mineral wool batts into the space between the wall studs. We've placed most of the studs at 16" (40 cm) on center spacing, which gives us 14 ½" (37 cm) of space between the studs. The mineral wool batts come in different sizes, but get the 15 ¼" (40cm) wide type. It will fit tightly into your space and will be much easier to keep in one place. Make sure to get the insulation into every little nook and cavity. Your walls are exposed only once; this is the time to do it right.

2. If you have trouble keeping the mineral wool in place, use a string and a staple gun method. Create a zigzagging string structure between two studs to hold the mineral wool in place. It is especially useful in ceiling and insulated roofs. Sauna insulation goes in very quickly, and our sauna is so small that you are already finished before you start getting bored.

Sauna Vapor Barrier

As the name suggests, the vapor barrier prevents the vapor from penetrating the walls. We don't want any moisture in walls because moisture conducts heat, and if the mineral wool absorbs even a small bit of moisture, it loses its insulating properties. For standard construction applications, we use polyethylene membrane. This can be used in changing rooms and other rooms that do not experience high temperatures in a sauna building.

For sauna use, Aluminum with a paper backing membrane should be used. This material is suitable for sauna temperatures, and there is no risk of melting or off-gassing. Additionally, an aluminum membrane reflects heat radiating from the sauna back inside.

ACTION:

Tools:

- 16GA finishing nailer
- Measuring Tape
- Spirit level

Materials:

- Aluminum-paper vapor membrane
- Self-adhesive Aluminum foil

1. Line the walls and the ceiling with this membrane, making sure to overlap any joints by at least 4" (100 mm).

2. Use a self-adhesive Aluminum tape to tape over the places where 2 membranes meet.

3. Make sure you check for any accidental punctures and tape them too. It's extremely important to get this membrane airtight because any leaks will cause moisture to enter the insulating layer (mineral wool), greatly reducing its insulating properties. The inside of your sauna should look like an aluminum-clad spaceship.

Applying the paper-backed Aluminum vapor membrane. Notice the additional blocking for the wall-hung heater and the air channel underneath.

Taping over the seams.

Air Gap

An air gap behind your interior sauna paneling is essential to allow for air to circulate behind it. The air helps to dry out the timber from behind and prolongs its life. If you leave no air gap, you are increasing the chance of wood rot. You might be fine if you use wood that is more resistant to rot, like western red cedar, but I would strongly consider it as the air gap. It is an inexpensive and quick way of improving your sauna.

Run laths through a table saw to create ½" to 1" (12 mm to 25 mm) wooden strips. Attach them on top of the Sauna vapor barrier vertically, in the places where there is framing behind. Use a pneumatic staple gun or hammer and nails. The ceiling should have an air gap, too. Make sure to add strips around the door so the edges support that wooden paneling.

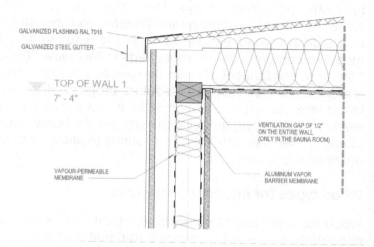

GALVANIZED FLASHING RAL 7016

GALVANIZED STEEL GUTTER

TOP OF WALL 1
7' - 4"

VENTILATION GAP OF 1/2"
ON THE ENTIRE WALL
(ONLY IN THE SAUNA ROOM)

VAPOUR-PERMEABLE
MEMBRANE

ALUMINUM VAPOR
BARRIER MEMBRANE

Detail section view through a wall, ceiling and roof of the sauna.

Internal Wall Paneling

The paneling stage is when your sauna interior finally starts looking like a sauna. The most often used wood type in North America is Western Red Cedar. It smells great, is resistant to moisture, and has a beautiful look. In Europe, the type of wood that is used for internal sauna paneling is spruce. It's widely available, inexpensive, and does the job well. It's more common for spruce to have knots, so you might need to handpick your boards. Knots are not great, as the hardwood in the center of the knot expands at a different rate when hot than all other wood, and this will cause the knot to be loose over time. Other types that are also used are Aspen, Alder, Abachi, and Magnolia. The same timber species but thermally modified are also a great choice, although they are more expensive.

The boards should be Tongue and Grove (T&G). It is a milled profile on each board length. It allows the next board to slot in and hides the gap. The boards need to be T&G because high humidity and temperature swings can cause the board to shrink more than normal. The tongue width is usually 1/3rd the thickness of the board. Whether you choose cedar or a different wood, ensure the timber is ready to use. The moisture content of the timber needs to be below 20%, and 15% or lower is ideal. Get an inexpensive wood moisture tester - it will also last you for future projects. If the wood is too wet, store it in a dry, covered, warm space for a few weeks. When drying timber, don't just put the boards on top of each other. Separate them with shims to allow air to pass between the boards.

Wood types for interior sauna walls

Wood for walls and benches is a natural choice for sauna construction. It is a hygroscopic material that can absorb humidity from the air. There is a significant increase in the surface temperature of the interior paneling when the Relative Humidity in the sauna room increases from pouring water on the hot sauna heater. This is beneficial for a sauna because we can easily regulate the amount of heat experienced just by pouring water. Wood also makes for a softer löyly. Because of the hygroscopic properties of wood, the humidity is absorbed and released slowly. If the walls were made from a non-permeable material like glass or ceramic tile, the experience of löyly (when you pour water on the stove) would be much more sudden, harsh, and unpleasant.

To select the right timber for your sauna, look at what's available in your location.

For interior walls, choose a soft wood type. Spruce, Pine, Cedar, and Abachi are popular choices.

North America	Europe / British Isles	Australasia
Eastern White Pine	Yellow pine	Aspen
Sugar Pine	European Spruce	Western yellow pine
Northern white cedar	European lime	Red cedar
Ponderosa pine	European Aspen	Western red cedar
Western red cedar	European red pine	Queensland's kauri pine
Incense cedar	Thermally modified variants of the above	Thermally modified variants of the above
Redwood		

For benches and backrest, I recommend selecting a higher-grade wood. Use finely sanded planks without knots, sap, or splinters. Abachi works really well, as well as Lime, Alder, Aspen, and Cedar.

ACTION:

Tools:

- Mitre saw

Materials:

- ¾" tongue and grove paneling - cedar or spruce

1. Start by laying your board flat and picking the best and worst. The best ones will go at eye level or where you might lean on them, and the worst boards can be used close to the floor where the imperfections won't be as noticeable.

2. Start with the bottom of the wall and work your way up. Measure the wall on the bottom, in the middle, and at the top. All three dimensions should be equal. Subtract a ¼" from these dimensions and start cutting the boards. The small gap will let the board shrink and expand, making the installation much easier. Ensure that the gap between the edge of the board and the Aluminum foil is less than the thickness of the boards. Leave a gap of around 1" (2.5 cm) from the floor and start your paneling there. The gap is necessary for the ventilation of paneling from behind.

3. Make sure the first board is perfectly level. If you want to conceal the nails, attach the boards by shooting the nails at a 45-degree angle through the tongue, which sticks up. Another method is the use of special metal brackets. The metal brackets are attached to the wall and hold up the boards. The advantage of this solution is that you can disassemble the paneling without damaging it.

4. When you reach the top of the wall, measure the remaining space and cut the last board so that around ½" (15mm) is left between the top of the board and the ceiling. This will allow the air to circulate behind the paneling. The small gap that's left over is not very pretty, but you can cover it up with the thickness of the ceiling paneling build-up.

The first internal siding board sits on top of 1" (3cm) timber blocks. The blocks are temporary. The distance created is perfect for pouring a thin concrete slab.

Fireproofing Heater Surroundings

A non-combustible wall surrounding your heater is a must. There have been way too many sauna fires caused by the ignition of timber siding around the heater. You may consider a brick masonry wall. This could work, but masonry is heavy and usually requires foundation. This would put unnecessary strain on our sauna. A great way to fireproof the surroundings of our heater is by sheathing the wall with a non-combustible Fiber cement board. It is strong, durable, and fireproof. Durarock is a brand name of fiber cement board available in the US. It is easy to cut my marking and scoring with a utility knife on one side, bending it and cutting from the other side. Read the instructions that came with your heater. Most manufacturers recommend around 7" (18 cm) of non-combustible material around the heater. This will determine the width of your cement board. I like to go all

the way to the ceiling. This provides a nice continuous surface and can be part of interior design. You can skim-coat
your fiber cement board with a thin cement coat or install a
natural stone tile - this is my preferred finish.

ACTION:

Tools:

- Angle grinder for cutting the Fiber cement board
- Notched Trowel
- Optional: Tile wedge, tile spacers
- Tape measure
- Spirit Level
- Face safety shield
- HEPA filter mask

Materials:

- Natural stone tiles
- Flexible tile adhesive
- Wood screws

1. Ensure there is blocking where the heater will be and
   that the Paper back Aluminum has been applied and
   taped properly.
2. Cut the fiber cement board to size. Depending on your
   heater, you will want about a 2' (60 cm) wide section.
3. Attach the cement board by using wood screws fas-
   tened directly into the wall studs.
4. Apply the finish you want: Either a cement skim coat or
   a natural stone tile. The stone tile can be attached with
   regular adhesive mortar, which is also used for ceramic
   tiles.

5. Mark out the mounting holes for your wall-hung sauna heater. Some manufacturers send a hole template that can easily mark out the holes.

6. The sauna heater should be attached as per the manufacturer's instructions. They usually specify the mounting system and the drill bit diameter.

If you plan on applying the skim coat finish method, it is best done by laying the cement board flat on a worktable. Before applying the skim coat, the cement board should be wet - use a damp sponge for this. The cement board and the skim coat will stick much better.

The contrast of dark, natural slate and Spruce wall paneling creates an accent wall.

Sauna Finished Floor

The sauna floor possesses a couple of unique construction challenges. The floor needs to withstand high humidity and high temperature, be slip-resistant, and be relatively light for a stick-framed floor. It is also important that a point drain is installed so that the floor can be washed with ease.

In my plans, I usually recommend the following floor layers:

Top

1. Epoxy
2. Fiber reinforced concrete
3. Waterproofing layer
4. Subfloor - moisture-resistant OSB or Plywood
5. Mineral wool between the framing members
6. Vapor-permeable air and water barrier
7. Animal control layer - stainless steel mesh or Exterior grade Plywood.

Bottom

The above layers result in a durable, slip-resistant, high temperature resistant floor that is excellent for outdoor saunas. Layers 1 and 2 can be replaced by ceramic or natural tile, but another layer of Fiber cement must be added to avoid cracking the tiles.

There are other ways to build the finished floor.

The second method is simple but effective. It is often used in Finland. The floor comprises wooden boards, with 1/4" (10mm) gaps between the boards. The gaps allow spilled water to be drained directly down to the ground. They also provide a source of fresh air. Below the wooden boards, you would only have the floor joists, with no additional membranes. This method introduces cold air at the bottom, so remember you will get a greater air stratification. The boards will last for years because there is plenty of ventilation around the wood.

The third method uses wooden boards for flooring, but the boards are tongue and groove and slope to a drain. I recommend Larch tongue and grove, around ⅞" (22mm) thick.

Larch is a durable wood and will last you for years. It is a preferred method of flooring in private saunas. It is not the best choice for public saunas because it's less durable than tile or concrete. Likewise, it's also great if you plan to transport your sauna. Wood is a flexible material, and when you transport your sauna by trailer or a crane, it will not crack. The boards can be angled down to a centrally located linear drain. The drain will have to sit between your floor joists.

Waterproof the OSB Subfloor with a liquid waterproofing membrane applied with a paint roller. Follow the manufacturer's guidelines for exact application and drying times. Cut the larch boards down to the required length. Ensure the length is about ¼" (0.6 cm) smaller than the wall-to-wall dimension to install the boards. Place a linear drain in the center of the sauna. Make sure the outlet is watertight and leads the water away from the sauna. The larch floor sits on shims that are shaped to give the floor a slope. The boards should be waterproofed by natural oil.

ACTION:

Tools:

- Concrete mixer
- Screed
- Float
- 360 Laser level
- Brush
- Roller

Materials:

- Concrete mixture
- Water
- Liquid waterproofing

- Corner waterproofing tape

1. Begin by installing the central drain P trap. The P trap should be the lowest part of your floor, and the surface of the floor should slope towards it.

2. If you haven't done it already, you must first make the floor waterproof. We will use liquid waterproofing, which you apply with a brush or a roller. First, paint the entire floor-to-wall connections. Next, we will want to give an extra waterproofing layer there because timber is flexible, and over time, a gap can form that lets the moisture penetrate our bottom wall plate. We will use a special corner waterproofing tape. Cut it to size and place it in all the corners. Apply another layer of waterproofing on top of it. We will then paint on a waterproofing layer with a roller brush on the whole floor and let it dry. Wait for it to cure (usually a couple of hours, but read the instructions).

3. Mark the high level on the walls to achieve the slope you want. An extremely useful tool for this is a 360-degree laser level. It's a device that shoots, you guessed it, a laser all around it. You will get a continuous laser line that is exactly level. Transfer it onto the wall using a pencil and a straight edge. You will want enough height to achieve a minimum slope of 1 degree. The slab should be 1" (2.5 cm) thick at the absolute minimum. For simplicity, we will mark a line that's 2 ½" (6 cm) off the ground, and the floor drain will be set at around 1 ½" (4 cm) above the subfloor. This will give us plenty of slope and enough concrete to make it solid.

4. The last thing we must do before concrete work is to create a flexible gap between the concrete and the walls. Timber and concrete expand at different rates, and this can cause concrete cracking. Install a 3" (7.5cm) strip of foam tape - a special product used for this application. The tape allows for the concrete to expand freely. The tape can be attached with a staple gun. The excess can be trimmed after the concrete cures.

5. Finally, mix up a batch of concrete to cover the floor with roughly 2 ½" (6 cm). Mixing up more than you need is better because we want to pour the floor in one go.

6. Pour the concrete, starting from the furthest corner, and work your way towards the door. As you pour the concrete, begin shaping it, so there is a gentle slope towards the drain. It will be tricky at first, but you must be patient. While the concrete is still fresh, use a trowel to do diagonal expansion joints. Essentially, it's another way to prevent cracking. They can be easily done by running a trowel vertically, on a diagonal, from the corner of your sauna to the floor drain.

7. Finish off pouring the whole floor and admire your work. Let it cure overnight. When you begin working the next day, be careful because concrete needs a few more days to achieve its full hardness.

8. To finish the floor, cut off the excess expansion foam tape and fill the diagonal expansion joints with a silicone filler.

9. The last thing to do is to seal the concrete. Do this after at least a week (longer in cold weather). To seal concrete, you can use clear floor epoxy. You basically paint it on with a roller and let it dry.

That's it, you have a nice, solid, waterproof floor. This is one of those things that you will appreciate after years of sauna use.

Installation of an Electrical Heater

Every heater is different, and I always recommend adhering to the manufacturer's guidelines when installing an electric or wood heater. One really important thing is to ensure minimum fire safety distances. For the purpose of this book, we assume you are installing a wall-mounted heater.

Safety distances

A	120 mm	4.8 in
B	630 mm	24.8 in
C	455 mm	17.9 in
D	190 mm	7.5 in
E	min 310 mm	min 12.2 in

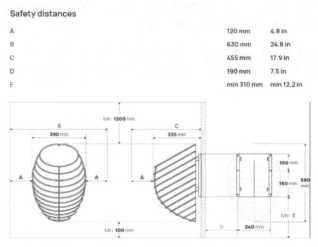

An example of the mounting specifications from a supplier. A wall-hung model from HUUM, an Estonian manufacturer, is shown in this case.

Check the mounting holes' position in the manufacturer's documentation. Mark out the location of the mounting holes on the wall. Make sure the heater is level and in the position you want. Pre-drill the holes with an appropriately sized drill bit diameter selected. The electric heater should be connected with a SiHf (silicone) high-temperature wire. If a three-phase connection powers your heater, the wire should have 5 smaller wires inside. I strongly recommend leaving electrical connections to a qualified electrician to ensure full compliance with local regulations and ensure insurance coverage should there be an issue.

Making the Sauna Benches

The sauna benches can be made as a separate structure bolted to the sauna walls, or they can be made in their final position. I prefer the first option, as the tight interior of the sauna makes it more difficult to work. We will make the benches 24" wide (60 cm). It is the ideal width for laying down. The length of the benches will be determined by measuring the distance from one side of the sauna to the other (after installing the paneling) and subtracting ¼" (0.6 cm) from it. The ¼" gap will let us install the benches easily. Otherwise, the fit would be too tight.

I will show two separate designs. They will differ in the way timber is used. The first design will use big solid 2x4s of fine quality without any knots. Timber like this is sometimes difficult to find, so buying 1" (25-28 mm) planks specially prepared for sauna benches is common. The structure of the bench is then made from ordinary 2x4 framing timber.

Sauna Benches Dimensions

The dimensions below are what is comfortable for most people. Use them to design your own benches.

	Metric	Imperial

From the top bench to the ceiling	100-120cm	3'4" to 4"
Bench height	40-48 cm	16" to 19"
Step riser	30-35 cm	12" to 14"
Step run	25-35 cm	10" to 14"
Bench with per person	60 cm	2'
Foot bench room	>30 cm	>1'
Bench depth, seated	45-60 cm	3' to 3'4"

Suggested measurements for different bench segments from "The secrets of Finnish Sauna Design" by L. Likkanen in 2021

A good way to design the benches is to start from the ceiling and design down. Measure 39" to 47" (100 cm to 120 cm) down from the ceiling. This is where your top bench will be. Measure another 19" (48 cm). This is where the lower bench is. Measure the remaining distance. If it's 19", great! If it's more than 19" you will have to build few steps.

Rise should be around 6" (15 cm), and going should be around 9" (23 cm). All the steps should have equal height. There is a handy formula that architects use to design comfortable stairs.

2H+D= 24 to 26"

H = Height, D= Depth

For example, for steps that are 6" high and 10", the formula is (2*6") +10" = 24." These steps would tick the box.

Sauna Benches Layout

The internal layout of the benches should meet the demands of the sauna benches' Dimensions. There are endless possibilities for placing benches in relation to each other, but most of the time, people choose one of the four ways described below.

The layouts' names are based on their shape when looking from above.

"I" layout - benches against the back wall

"L" layout - two benches at 90 degrees to each other

"II" layout - two benches opposite each other

"U" layout - 3 benches in a U shape

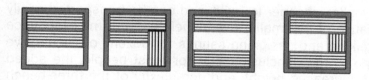

The most common and simplest to build is the "I" layout, which we will build in the later chapters. This layout is basic but also functional. Two or more benches are up against a wall, with a heater opposite. This also allows a big picture window. You should stick with this layout unless you have a strong reason to do a different layout.

The "L" layout is often considered, but it creates an awkward corner where the space is unusable. The "U" layout is a combination of "L" and "I" layouts. It comes with similar issues regarding the unusable corners, but it gives more overall seating space. Use it if your space is limited, but you want more people using your sauna. The "II" model is good, but you force people to look at each other. This can be good - it can get people talking to each other and is the more 'social' layout. Not all people will like this layout. Some prefer a sauna as a calming and meditative experience.

The benches can also be staggered. If you go with an "L" layout, the benches on one wall can be lowered by half the bench height. This would create a layout with 'half levels,' allowing you to choose height more precisely.

Two or three bench levels?

There have been countless debates online on the topic of two vs three bench levels in a sauna. If you are the kind of person who reads the fine print on the back of every food item, then you will want to go with the three-level layout. The three bench levels satisfy the law of Löyly - feet above the stones (more on that later). The two-bench level design does not satisfy this law, but on the other hand, the building is smaller, cheaper to build, and can be transported easily because of its smaller overall height. From my experience of talking and designing saunas for dozens of clients, I've come to the conclusion that for most people, the added cost, increased height, and complexity of the three-bench level are not worth it. People just want a sauna and are fine with a two-bench level sauna, even if they know the 3-bench level design is superior. Not everyone needs a Mercedes - for most people, a Toyota is fine.

Sauna Benches - Materials

The material of the benches is traditionally wood. Wood is a good insulator and does not conduct heat well. In a sauna, this is exactly what we want. You could easily burn your skin if another material like steel or tile was used. There are many species of wood with various properties. The required properties of a sauna bench material are relatively light. Durable, knot-free, sap-free, non-hazardous, not prone to splintering, dimensional stability.

Some types that are common in Europe are Thermopine, Red Cedar (Thuja Plicata), Monterey pine (pine radiata), Alder, Lime tree, knot, and sap-free spruce (Picea abies).

In North America, a common choice is Western Red Cedar, Sugar Pine, White cedar, and Eastern white pine.

First bench design

The first design integrates the frame structure with the timber you sit on.

The benches will be 24" by 6' 5 ¾" (0.6 m by 2 m) in our design. Begin going to the wood supply store and hand-select the finest 2x4s you can find. The species of timber should be Western Red Cedar. You can also choose Aspen, Alder, or Abachi, but this timber is usually harder to find. Trim the ends to get a square edge before cutting the boards to their final size.

The materials needed (below are the actual dimensions) :

- 7 pieces of 6' 2½" x 3 ½" x 1 ½" (189cm x 9.5cm x 4.5cm)
- 2 pieces of 24" x 3 ½" x 1 ½" (60cm x 9.5cm x 4.5cm)
- 5 pieces of 1'9" x 1 ¾" x 1 ¾" (51cm x 4.5cm x 4.5cm)

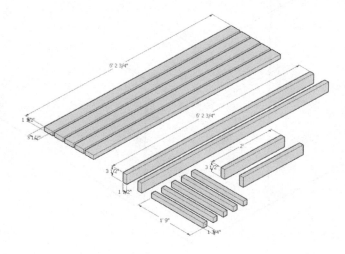

Lay the 4 boards as per the image below like a picture frame. Pre-drill the holes to attach the shorter and longer boards together. Use carpenter's clamps to secure the 'frame' temporarily when you screw it together.

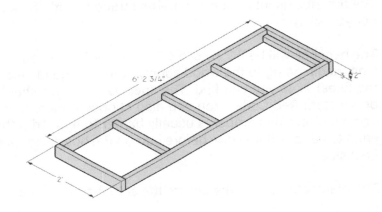

Axonometric view of the bench frame

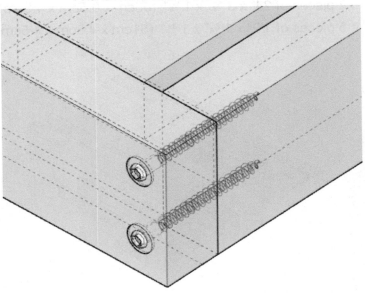

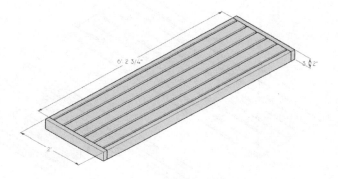

Detail Axonometric view of sauna frame connection. Countersunk Torx screws, 3 1/2" (90mm) long, ¼" (6.5mm) diameter

Finished sauna bench with dimensions

The boards that you sit on are attached by screwing in stainless steel screws from underneath. Make sure you pre-drill the holes and that the screws do not protrude through the boards. They should be at least ¼" (6 mm) shorter so they do not go through.

Alternative bench design

The second design will use thinner planks (around ¾" to 1" or 20 - 28mm) as the finished surface. The boards are too thin to provide strong support, so the frame needs to be stronger. We will use 2x4's (95 x 45 mm) as a structural frame. Every 12 to 16" (30-40 cm), there should be cross bracing. The ideal width of sauna bench boards is 3" (75 mm) with about ¾" (25 mm) gaps between. The boards are wide enough to be comfortable, and the gaps provide a sufficient gap for air to pass through and decrease the air stratification.

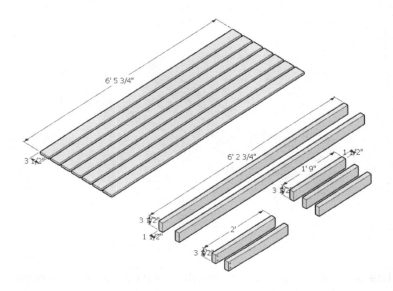

Components needed for the alternative bench design.

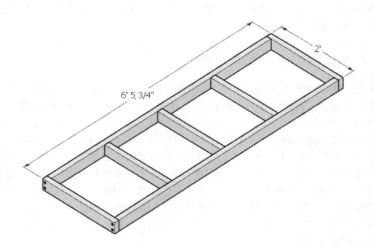

The pre-assembled frame.

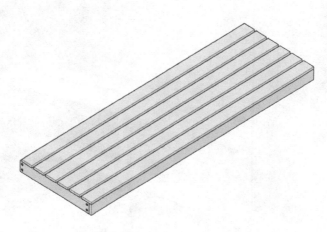

The finished sauna bench

Bench support can be done by screwing 2x4 timber supports into the wall and then resting the finished benches on top of them. It's also good to create vertical legs (marked orange in the diagram below) that support the center of the benches.

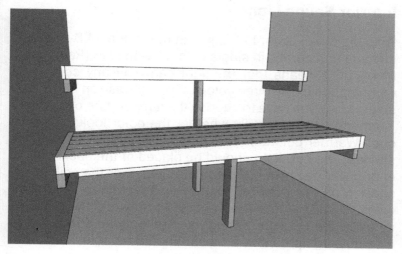

Bench support

Chapter 4 | Sauna Interior

The benches above were built completely in their final location. While this method is fine, prefabricating them in a different location would have been easier.

Interior Sauna Light

I'm a big fan of linear LED lights in the sauna. LED is energy efficient and comes in single color or with RGB (Red, Green, Blue). RGB means that the light can emit any color as a combination of the three colors. If you choose an LED with a single color, you have to choose the *temperature* of the light. Temperature is basically whether the color looks warm or cool. Warmer colors in the 2500-3500K range are ideal for saunas. The LED light should be placed at the backrest level or lower because high temperatures near the ceiling will shorten its life. An IP 67 waterproof Aluminum enclosure gives the LED strip a sturdy place to stay and the possibility to soften the light through a semi-opaque diffuser. Any electrical equipment in a sauna should be connected with heat-resistant silicone cable.

Ventilation

One of the final steps is to provide proper ventilation. As you learned from the "Sauna Design Principles" chapter, there are two main ways: Natural and Mechanical ventilation. We've discussed the pros and cons already, so I will let you decide which one to pick in the case of mechanical. The one main difference is that you will have more wiring for the mechanical fan. The Intake and exhaust cutting are similar in both versions.

Here, I will describe the process of Natural ventilation, as the barrier of entry is lower, and it will allow more people to complete the build. Mechanical ventilation provides better results with less heat layering, so if you have skills, time, and patience, go with that.

ACTION:

Tools:

- Cordless drill
- Jigsaw
- Hand wood file
- Knife for mineral wool

Materials:

- Flexible 4"(100 mm) diameter aluminum ventilation duct. Vent covers - one timber and two metal.

1. Locate the intake and exhaust vent placement. The intake should be located under or beside the heater. If it is located under the heater, the height of the opening is determined by the heater itself. Aim for about 12" or 30cm from the finished floor. The exhaust should be on a wall on the opposite side of the sauna from the heater, about 6" (15 cm) from the ceiling. The main thing is to miss

the wall studs and the battens - you don't want to drill through them. Also, if you can, try to locate your vents in the centerline of your internal boards.

2. Locate the center of the duct and mark out the diameter with a compass. Drill holes on the inside of the perimeter of the duct. This will make the next step easier.

3. Carefully use a jigsaw to cut the circle out. Stay on the inside of the diameter when cutting. If you cut the vent under the heater, the round vent might not fit. In this case, cut a rectangular vent with the same profile area so that it is round.

4. The remaining part can be removed with a hand file or a Dremel tool. There are also special drill sanding attachments that you can use for this step.

5. Cut the opening in the Vapor barrier with a utility knife.

6. Cut the opening in mineral wool with a long knife. There are special knives for cutting mineral wool.

7. Cut an opening in a Vapor permeable membrane.

8. Hopefully, you did not encounter any studs. Battens are mostly fine; you can do a little bit of batten framing on the exterior to support the siding. If you encountered a wall stud, I'd recommend relocating the vent.

9. The last thing to cut is the external siding. This might be tricky to do from the outside because you have to locate the center of the duct. Here is what I recommend: Find the longest drill bit you can find and drill a hole in the center of the duct in the external siding from the inside of the sauna. Now that you have the center point, follow the procedure above to cut a hole in the siding.

10. Insert the flexible round aluminum vent duct. It should be held tightly by the mineral wool.

11. Seal the gaps between the round duct and the vapor barriers on the inside and the outside. Use self-adhesive tapes made from the same materials.

12. Install the vent covers. A mechanism on the inside should allow you to control the airflow. I prefer to control the exhaust. A round timber vent that you can screw in and screw out, or a sliding valve, is sufficient.

13. On the Outside, install powder-coated metal covers that match the diameter of your vent holes.

If you installed a fiber cement board and natural stone, you would have a harder time drilling the hole, but there is nothing a diamond hole drill bit can't shew through. Other steps are pretty much the same.

Finishing Touches

Window and Door finish trim

The window and door trim hide any inaccuracies from our sight. A trim is essentially a ' picture frame around our door or window. You are fine without it; it's just an extra step that can be taken. Depending on the desired effect, there are many ways to do the trim. Some can be minimalistic; others can be more traditional.

The most basic trim is done by creating a simple picture frame. The corners are done by joining two board cuts at a 45-degree angle. You can get trim stock ready to go or create your own by cutting off the tongue and groove on a table saw. By creating your own trim, you can save money and match exactly the material to your internal siding.

The door trim is usually made bigger by about ⅛" (0,12). This is called a reveal, and its purpose is to hide the small inaccuracies - they are harder to spot.

ACTION:

Tools Needed:

- Mitre saw
- Finish Nailer
- Shims
- Table saw

Materials needed:

- ¾" x 6" cedar siding

1. Measure the required length of trim for all your doors and windows.
2. Set aside the same length of 1" x6" paneling.
3. Set the table saw to cut the tongues off and cut them off from all the boards.
4. Do the same for the grooves.
5. Use a tape measure to set up the table saw to cut the board into halves. Cut the boards into halves - this will give you roughly 2 ½" wide trim stock.
6. Measure and cut the left and right sides of your door trim. It should go from the floor to the top of the door and add ⅛" for reveal.
7. Move the trim away ⅛" from the edge and set the trim in place with a finish nailer.
8. Measure the distance required for the top trim. Cut the trim to size and install it.

Trimming of the windows is pretty similar, except you will add a bottom trim. Additionally, there will be a window sill. On the outside, the window sill should be angled away from the building. You can create that angle by cutting ½" shims and moving them up close to the wall. To finish off the windows, I like to add a 'window box' or casing. It is essentially a 4 walled box (without the top and bottom). The dimensions should be taken around the window, and the box should be flush with the rough opening. You can use a finish nailer to secure the sides together, then set it in place, again using the finishing nailer.

Backrest

The backrest should be fabricated as a separate object and mounted in place when finished. First, fabricate the backrest brackets as per the diagram below. The 15-degree angle is optimal for comfort. You will need 4 brackets in total. The backrest bracket will have the same planks that you used for the benches. Three boards if the perfect amount - the middle board will cover the LED and produce a nice and diffused light. Make sure to attach the planks from behind. The metal parts can't be exposed. If you are working with Thermo wood, it's a good idea to pre-drill holes, as Thermo wood is dry and brittle. Make sure the brackets are spaced out so that they are aligned with wall studs. Install the LED Aluminum enclosure in the backrest bracket cutouts. Install the pre-assembled backrest in the correct location on the back wall (check the height to suit you). To attach it to the wall, you can use the gaps between the planks to drive long screws through the backrest bracket and the wall framing.

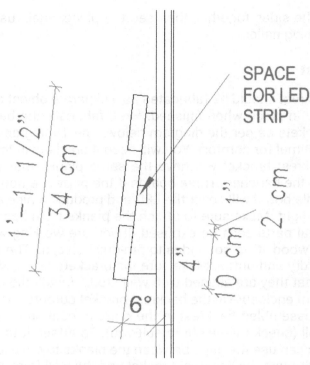

SPACE
FOR LED
STRIP

1' – 1 1/2"

34 cm

1"

2 cm

4"

10 cm

6°

Detail section of a back rest mounting

A simple design is sometimes the best

Wall hooks

Towel hooks are one of those small things that greatly enhance the sauna experience, yet we only notice them when they are missing. Hang up your robe, clothes, or an extra towel.

Some people might be fine with just using a finish nail as a hook. I like the idea of buying hooks that match the style of the sauna or light fixtures. If you go for round, matte black light fixtures, pick a towel hook that uses the same design language: Cylinders and matte black powder coat. Also, they are one of those details that will be exposed, so making a design decision and spending a few dollars here is worth it.

Pick a spot to hang them up that is comfortable for you. I would like to have hooks on the back wall of the changing room.

Stacking sauna stones

There are a couple of key rules that should be followed when stacking stones in your heater.

1. The stones should be pointing upward if they are elongated.
2. The stones should have some space between them to allow for air circulation.
3. Fit the stones between the heating elements only if the heater manufacturer recommends it. In some heaters, you are risking heating elements touching each other, so the stones are needed, but in other heaters, it's the exact opposite.
4. Fit as many stones as you can while respecting the above points.

CHAPTER 5
SUMMARY

What a journey this has been! You just went from a person who probably had zero experience in construction to hopefully a determined sauna builder.

At this point, you can consider a few extras that you could add to your sauna:

- Sound Systems: Waterproof speakers can add a whole new dimension. Imagine chilling to your favorite tunes or the soothing sounds of nature.

- Aromatherapy: Add a few drops of essential oils to the water for an enhanced sensory experience.

- Cooling Off Area: Complete your setup with a plunge pool or an outdoor shower. There's nothing like that invigorating cool down after a hot sauna.

Building your sauna will be a journey of passion, patience, and a bit of sweat equity. Every time you step inside, you'll not only enjoy the benefits but also feel a surge of pride. Here's to many sessions of good heat, good steam, and the satisfaction of a job well done. Enjoy the heat, the relaxation, and every drop of sweat that signifies your hard-earned accomplishment.

Sauna Maintenance

Sauna maintenance is crucial to its longevity. It's also a matter of hygiene. Take care of your sauna, and it will last you for years.

Exterior

Roof Inspection:

- Regularly check the roof for signs of corrosion, wear, and leaks. Water is the primary enemy of any structure.
- Ensure that any roofing materials are intact and properly sealed to prevent water ingress.

Timber Facade Care:

- Maintain the external timber facade with the products it was originally treated with, or follow the manufacturer's recommendations.
- If you used the Shou Sugi Ban method and oiled the boards, re-apply the oil every couple of years to protect the wood and maintain its appearance.

Interior

Clean the windows as needed. I recommend quickly mopping the sauna floor after each sauna use.

Perform a deep clean with natural, wood-safe soap a few times a year, depending on how frequently the sauna is used. This helps keep the wood looking fresh and hygienic.

After each sauna session, open the top vent to allow moisture to escape. Leave the door slightly open to speed up the drying process. This helps prevent mold and mildew by removing excess moisture.

Heater

Heating elements in sauna heaters are considered consumable, so get spares in advance. Check the heating elements for any signs of wear or damage. Replace any elements that are not working properly.

Stones

Sauna stones should be checked at least once a year. Replace the cracked and brittle ones. The minerals in the water that you use to create löyly can sometimes leave a small residue on the surface of the stones. This is completely natural - it is usually the high level of calcium present that is causing it. The stones that have a visible layer of deposit should be replaced. It is usually the stones at the top of the heater that suffer the most. When you do your yearly stone replacement, take out around 80% of the stones from your heater. Replace the brittle, cracked ones or the ones with residue.

Need more info?

Comprehensive sauna plans

Get instant access to comprehensive sauna plans, complete with detailed sections, elevations, and a bill of materials. Browse our website at homemadesauna.com to explore a wide variety of sauna designs and find the perfect one for you.

Custom Sauna Design and Project Management Package

If you're seeking a sauna that's tailored to your unique needs and preferences, our custom sauna design and project management package is the perfect solution.

Tailored to Your Vision

I will work closely with you to bring your vision to life, taking into account factors such as:

- Size and layout of your space
- Personal style
- Budget

Comprehensive Package

With our comprehensive package, which is available for review on our website, you'll receive customized design concepts, detailed project plans, and expert guidance throughout the entire process.

If you made it here, congratulations! I hope you are now confident with your sauna project. If you have any feedback about this book or if I got anything wrong, please let me know at contact@homemadesauna.com

**If you managed to build your sauna,
I would love to see some photos!**

CHAPTER 6
BONUS CHAPTER: HOW TO START YOUR SAUNA BUSINESS

Now that you've invested time and resources into building your dream sauna, you can consider turning your passion into a thriving business. Renting out your sauna can help offset the construction costs while allowing you to share the joy of sauna bathing with others in your community. Many sauna enthusiasts have successfully transformed their backyard saunas into profitable ventures, and with the right approach, you can, too.

My parents took this approach when they built their own outdoor sauna. To offset the costs, they decided to rent it out to the local community. It proved to be a wonderful supplementary income, allowing them to constantly improve the sauna experience. Over time, it has become their passion to create a welcoming and relaxing space for all who visit.

Location is key when starting a sauna business. If you're building a stationary sauna, ensure it complies with local zoning laws and regulations. Consult with your building department about ADA accessibility requirements, necessary permits, and health and safety standards. Depending on your location, there may be specific guidelines and restrictions around operating a commercial sauna. Be sure to thorough-ly research the legal landscape before investing significant time and resources into your venture. Building a strong re-lationship with local county offices can help streamline the process and ensure you meet all necessary requirements.

Alternatively, a portable sauna on a trailer or heavy-duty frame offers more flexibility. This model allows you to avoid many regulatory hurdles while providing the freedom to set up shop in different locations. If you live in a tourist-heavy area, you're in luck - just be mindful of the competition and don't be afraid to establish your sauna rental near other pro-viders. If there's a lack of sauna offerings in your area, seize the opportunity to be a pioneer in that market!

Portable saunas open up a world of possibilities when it comes to location. You can set up shop at festivals, events, or even offer mobile sauna experiences for private parties and corporate events. This versatility allows you to reach a wider audience and tap into different revenue streams. However, be sure to carefully consider the logistics of trans-porting and setting up your sauna at various sites.

Business Model

Determine your target market (locals, tourists, events, etc.). Understanding your ideal customer will help you tai-lor your offerings and marketing efforts. Are you catering to health-conscious locals seeking a relaxing retreat, or do you envision hosting bachelorette parties and corporate team-building events?

Decide on a pricing structure (hourly, per person, group rates, etc.). Consider factors like the cost of utilities, mainte-nance, and any additional services you plan to offer. Hourly rates are common, but you could also offer package deals or discounts for larger groups.

Establish operating hours and availability. Will you be open year-round or seasonally? What days and times will you be available? Clearly communicating your hours of operation will help manage customer expectations and ensure a smooth booking process.

Customer Experience

Ensure the sauna is preheated and ready for guests' arrival. Nothing is more disappointing than arriving to a cold sauna. Develop a process for preheating the sauna well in advance so it's at the optimal temperature when your customers arrive.

Offer complimentary extras like hot tea or refreshments. Small touches like these can improve the overall experience and make your guests feel taken care of. This is the difference between no Reviews and a 5 star review on Google. Provide clean towels, robes, and a comfortable lounge area. Create a welcoming space for your guests to relax before and after their sauna session.

Ensure a seamless check-in and check-out process. Clearly communicate any rules or instructions and be available to answer questions.

Encourage positive reviews on platforms like Google Maps. Satisfied customers are your best marketing asset, so make it easy for them to leave glowing reviews that will attract new business.

Creating a memorable and comfortable customer experience is key to building a successful business and setting it apart from the competition. Ensure that guests feel well-informed and supported throughout their visit.

Legal and Compliance

Research the necessary business licenses and permits for your area. Depending on your location, you may need to obtain a general business license, sales tax permit, or other specific licenses related to operating a sauna facility.

Consider forming an LLC to protect your personal assets. A limited liability company (LLC) separates your business assets from your personal assets, providing an extra layer of protection in case of legal issues or lawsuits.

Obtain liability insurance to mitigate potential risks. Accidents can happen, and liability insurance will protect your business from financial loss in case someone is injured on your premises.

Ensure your facility meets ADA accessibility requirements. The Americans with Disabilities Act (ADA) mandates that public accommodations be accessible to individuals with disabilities. This may include requirements for parking spaces, entrances, and restroom facilities.

It's essential to ensure that your sauna facility complies with all relevant accessibility regulations. By prioritizing accessibility and compliance, you demonstrate a commitment to inclusivity and create a welcoming environment for all guests, while protecting yourself from any accidents or lawsuits.

Marketing and Branding

Analyze the competition's online reviews to identify areas where you can offer a superior service. Set up a Google Business profile to appear on Google Maps and drive new bookings. Create a user-friendly website with online booking capabilities using platforms like Squarespace or Wix. Spread the word through social media, host free sauna parties, and strategically place banners in high-traffic areas.

Your website should showcase your sauna experience, pricing, and booking information, while social media allows you to share updates promotions, and interact with your audience.

Leverage local listing platforms like Google My Business. Claiming and optimizing your Google My Business listing will help your sauna show up in local searches and make it easier for customers to find you.

Offer promotions or host free events to attract new customers. Consider offering discounts or free trial sessions to entice new customers to experience your sauna. You could also partner with local businesses or organizations to host events or wellness workshops, which can expose your business to a wider audience.

Distribute marketing materials (banners, flyers) in strategic locations. While digital marketing is crucial, don't underestimate the power of traditional marketing methods. Strategically placing banners or distributing flyers in high-traffic areas can grab the attention of potential customers who may not have discovered you online.

Effective marketing and branding are essential for attracting customers and building a strong reputation in the sauna rental industry. Start by researching your competitors' online reviews to identify areas where you can differentiate your business and provide an exceptional customer experience. Claim and optimize your Google Business profile to ensure your sauna appears in local search results and on Google Maps, making it easy for potential customers to find and book your services.

Funding and Costs

As your business grows, consider hiring a backup person to assist with hosting duties. Negotiate a fair salary, typically

30% of the rental price. Provide them with detailed step-by-step procedures and hands-on training to ensure a smooth operation in your absence.

Starting a sauna rental business requires an upfront investment, from the initial construction costs to ongoing operational expenses. As your business expands, you may need to hire additional staff to assist with hosting duties and ensure smooth operations, especially during peak periods or when you're unavailable.

Estimate startup costs (licenses, insurance, marketing, etc.). Before launching your sauna business, it's essential to have a clear understanding of the costs involved. This may include licensing fees, insurance premiums, marketing expenses, and any necessary renovations or equipment purchases.

Sauna Construction and Material Sourcing

Ensure your sauna is safe, functional, and well-maintained. If you followed the previous chapters, this should already be taken care of.

Constructing a high-quality, safe, and functional sauna is the foundation of your rental business. If you have followed the guidance provided in the previous chapters of this book, you should have a well-designed and properly built sauna that meets all necessary safety standards. However, it's crucial to regularly maintain and inspect your sauna to ensure it continues to operate efficiently and safely for your guests.

If you have access to local wood or woodworking tools, then consider sourcing your materials locally to save on costs. Milling your own wood can significantly reduce costs, as well as cutting and finishing the wood product. If you do go this route, make sure to have your sauna designs before you mill. This way, you will know exactly how many and what type of cuts to mill.

Your Purpose

Define your purpose for starting a sauna business.

Beyond the financial motivations, what is the deeper meaning behind your sauna venture?

Do you want to promote wellness and relaxation in your community?

Or perhaps you envision creating a unique gathering space for people to connect and socialize?

Identify what fuels your passion for sauna bathing. Whether it's the therapeutic benefits, the cultural traditions, or simply the enjoyment of the sauna experience, understanding your personal motivations will help shape your business's identity and appeal to like-minded individuals.

Align your business goals with your personal values and vision. Ensure that your sauna business reflects your core values and beliefs. This authenticity will resonate with customers and help you build a loyal following.

Build a strong brand identity around your unique purpose. Develop a compelling brand story that communicates your purpose and values. This will help you stand out in a crowded market and attract customers who share your vision.

Scaling Your Sauna Rental Business

As your sauna business grows, continuously explore additional marketing channels like Google Ads, Facebook Ads, and partnerships with local vacation rental owners. Staying ahead of the curve and adapting to changing trends is essential for long-term success.

Remember, word-of-mouth is invaluable in the sauna business, so prioritize customer satisfaction and create memorable experiences that keep people coming back. Encourage feedback and be open to making improvements based on customer suggestions. By consistently delivering a high-quality sauna experience and staying true to your purpose, you'll build a loyal customer base and a thriving sauna business.

Starting a sauna business is not just about making money - it's about sharing your love for saunas and helping others experience the transformative benefits of this ancient wellness practice. With dedication, creativity, and a commitment to excellence, your sauna rental venture can become a thriving business and a fulfilling passion project.

AUTHOR BIOGRAPHY

Wojciech Kumik has been working in the Design industry, specifically in Architecture, for more than 8 years. He completed his Bachelor of Architecture at the University of Limerick in Ireland and Universidad San Jorge in Spain. Since 2019, he has been sharing his knowledge with students studying Home Design at Tischner European University in Kraków, Poland. From 2020 onwards, he has been creating outdoor saunas through his brand, Home Made Sauna (www.homemadesauna.com), assisting numerous individuals and a few companies in the US and Europe with their sauna design needs. Along with his wife, Iwona, he maintains a blog that is widely recognized as a valuable resource for Sauna construction.

LITERATURE

1. Rafter spans
   https://www.mycarpentry.com/rafter-span-tables.html

2. (IRC) International Residential Code Roof Ceiling Construction
   https://codes.iccsafe.org/content/IRC2021P2/chapter-8-roof-ceiling-construction#IRC2021P2_Pt03_Ch08_SecR802.4.1

3. Snow loads map in US
   https://www.dlubal.com/en/load-zones-for-snow-wind-earthquake/snow-global-figure-7-2-1.html?&center=40.68063802521456,-79.18945312500001&zoom=5&marker=38.888571,-77.05198#&center=42.46729758290374,-94.01448971962937&zoom=6&marker=38.888571,-77.05198.

4. Indoor Air Quality and Ventilation at Home A HANDBOOK TO SUPPORT EVERYDAY LIFE by The Organization for Respiratory Health in Finland
   https://www.hengitysliitto.fi/wp-content/uploads/2021/10/IlmanvaihtoOpas_2021_englanti_saavuttettava.pdf

5. 'The Secrets of Finnish Sauna Design' by Lassi A. Liikkanen

6. https://architektura.info/prawo/warunki_techniczne_
budynki/dzial_iv_wyposazenie_techniczne_budynkow/
rozdzial_6_wentylacja_i_klimatyzacja

7. https://www.e3s-conferences.org/articles/e3sconf/
pdf/2019/37/e3sconf_clima2019_02015.pdf

ACKNOWLEDGMENTS

Iwona Kumik - My wife has been very helpful during the time I was writing the book. Iwona gave me feedback in the initial phases of the book and helped with finding types and places where I didn't explain things well enough. She also helped with spreading the word about this book and setting up the marketing for it.

Grzegorz Kumik- I'm lucky to have a dad who is an Engineer and has more than 30 years of experience in Electrical projects, DIY and Construction. Greg and I built the very first sauna where we tested a lot of the techniques described here. Greg also helped with the Electrical chapter and made sure I didn't miss anything.

Marcus Del Bianco - proofreading & ideas for the bonus chapter

Graham Macnish - Proofreading

Danny Decilis - Beta reading and initial critique

Pooja Yadav - Line editing

HMDPUBLISHING - Book layout

URGENT PLEA!

Thank you for reading my book!

I really appreciate your feedback and I love hearing what you have to say.

I need your input to make the next version of this book and my future books even better.

Please take two minutes now to leave a helpful review letting me know what you thought of the book.

A review can be sent in by email to contact@ homemadesauna.com, or if you bought the book through Amazon, you can leave a review there.

Additional resources, including PDF of plan and section, can be obtained homemadesauna.com/pages/ ebook-resources

Made in the USA
Monee, IL
04 December 2024

72362272R00075